ARIZONA COWBOYS

SALT RIVER CROSSING.

Arizona
COWBOYS

DANE COOLIDGE

With Photographs by the Author

THE UNIVERSITY OF ARIZONA PRESS
Tucson, Arizona

About the Author

DANE COOLIDGE (1873–1940) was an itinerant photographer and writer who traveled throughout the American West, recording native wildlife and the developing frontier. In 1903 his wanderings brought him to the Verde River Valley of central Arizona, where he wrote the stories and took the photographs that comprise *Arizona Cowboys*. He was the author of numerous magazine pieces and books, among them *Old California Cowboys* and *Texas Cowboys*.

THE UNIVERSITY OF ARIZONA PRESS

Second printing 1989
Manufactured in the U.S.A.

Library of Congress Cataloging in Publication Data

Coolidge, Dane, 1873-1940.
Arizona cowboys.

Reprint. Originally published: New York: Dutton, 1938.
1. Cowboys—Arizona—Verde River Valley—History.
2. Frontier and pioneer life—Arizona—Verde River Valley. 3. Ranch life—Arizona—Verde River Valley.
4. Verde River Valley (Ariz.)—Social life and customs.
I. Title.
F817.V37C66   1984   979.1'57   83-27439
ISBN 0-8165-0858-5

Contents

List of Illustrations

9

Illustrations

ARIZONA COWBOYS

Chapter 1

CACTUS COWBOYS

THE first cattle in Arizona came from Mexico, like the longhorns, but they are a different breed from the Texas cows that stocked the Central Plains. Their horns are shorter and hooked straight back and, after running wild on the desert for two hundred years, they are dangerous to a man on foot. They are fighters and the cowboys who handle them have learned to use a sixty-foot rope.

They take a "dally" around the saddle-horn, so they can turn him loose quick, and leave the crazy idea of tying their rope for people like the Texans. With cattle like these it is necessary to have a mount that will obey, and they use the Spanish bit, the cruelest in the world. The spurs of those early-day *vaqueros* measured six inches across the rowels, and when they jabbed their horse in the belly he flew.

The modern Arizona cowboys use about the same rigging, only their spurs are not quite so large, and at roping they beat the world. But they do not give their horses their heads, like the Texans, and make a sport out of riding bronks. Their *caballos* are broken with a rawhide hackamore, which teaches them to answer to the reins long before they have a bit in their mouth, and

13

they fasten their reins together in a long bridle-lash or *romal* that can be hung over the horn when not in use.

Those old-time *vaqueros* had a way of their own for handling horses and cattle, and it must have had its points for it has been adopted all over the Far West, from California to the Rockies. Even the early settlers from Texas seem to have followed the custom of the country, and over all that vast range the cowboys still ride single-cinch saddles, take their turns around the horn when they rope and wear *tapaderas* on their stirrups. They hang chains on their spurs, to clank as they jog along, and have a weakness for silver-mounted bits and fancy rigging.

The Arizona cowboy was raised in a cactus patch and on a bet has been known to climb a giant cactus — touch a match to the long rows of spines and, after they burn off, swarm right up with his closed *chaparreras*. His horse, too, was raised in the cactus belt — anywhere south of the Mogollon Rim — and so were the hard-mouthed cows. It is difficult to believe it, but in times of drouth they actually eat cactus. All except the fuzzy *chollas*, whose fine thorns will kill the hardiest of them.

But they do not eat cactus because they like it. Every spine and tiny sticker, besides being barbed, is tipped with a poisonous venom as painful as the sting of a wasp. It makes a wound that swells and throbs and is slow to heal, but the cattle have to endure it. After breaking

JOSEFO.
An old-time Mexican *vaquero*.

A Tree Cholla.

In times of drouth the cattle break through these spines and eat off the joints from behind.

through the outer defences of a tree-cactus they eat it out from behind, then lie down with their noses stuck full of spiny joints and chew their cuds complacently. The inside of their mouths becomes as tough as India rubber, and if they can get enough water to dilute the bitter juice they will live on cactus a long time.

Not until the big mining strike at Tombstone, in 1878, did men like John Slaughter bring in Texas cattle for beef. They stayed then, for the Sulphur Springs Valley was a sea of waving grass; but it was not long until this same John Slaughter was going down into Sonora for his herds. The Texas steers were being driven north to the open ranges of Wyoming and Montana, and it was only an accident which turned them west — in 1885. A quarantine had been declared against all Texas cattle on account of the fever tick, and forty thousand head were diverted at one time into northern Arizona.

Cattle-train after cattle-train pulled into Holbrook and Winslow, and before snow fell there were long-horned steers from Flagstaff to the New Mexico line. It was a Texas invasion, and those first cowboys turned the country into a rustlers' paradise. If ever a range was ruled by rustlers it was the land on both sides of the Santa Fe Railroad, where the Aztec Land and Cattle Company owned every alternate township. In fourteen years there was not a single conviction for cattle-steal-

15

ing, and the cowthieves were shipping them out by the trainload.

But this was in the north, and the rustlers were Texans. South of the Mogollon Plateau, in the hot desert part of Arizona, the cattle business was going on as it had been for two hundred years — since Father Kino brought in seven hundred head and turned them loose at San Xavier de Bac. Old-timers say the grass used to be belly-deep on the level floor of the desert, but range conditions had changed when I went to my first rodeo at Pinal.

It was in 1903, and that winter it had forgotten to rain. This applied to most any of the previous ten winters, but that year had been special. It was the beginning of a drouth and if the cattlemen could have looked ahead another year they would have curled up and died, like the grass. The cattle ate cactus until they learned to like it and, believe it or not, for thirteen months it never rained a drop.

In February the cows were too thin to be chased, and there was no grass to feed the beef herd. So the men who owned the cattle that ran along Queen Creek put off the round-up a month. When the first of March came the grass was still too short. On the first of April they suddenly decided that it was not going to rain at all, and they had better gather their cattle right away before the calves left their mothers and the summer

16

heat came on. So the word was passed around in Tempe, where most of them lived, and I caught a ride out on a freight-wagon.

The first man to start was Mike McGrew, the freighter, with his lead wagon full of flour and bacon and his trail wagon loaded with grain and baled hay. The water was running bank-high in the ditches of the Salt River Valley, irrigating miles and miles of alfalfa; but when we crossed the last canal east of Mesa, we landed in the middle of a desert. Several hundred years before, as their old ditches showed, the Toltecs had watered all that country; but now only a forest of giant cacti gave evidence of its fertility. It was dry as a bone and barren as the Sahara, but that was nothing to Mc-Grew.

Twice a month for seventeen years he had toiled out across that desert to the old mining camp of Pinal — tugging along through the sand, then grinding up over the rocks, eighty miles without a free drink. On the first night we camped at Desert Well, where the water was ten cents a head. Another day of heat and dust and we pulled in to Whitlow's Well, where a crazy Dutchman tried to collect two bits a head. Ten cents was all McGrew would pay, but we had to pump the water ourselves.

On the third day we dragged up an endless canyon, where on many a black point the rocks had been piled

17

up to make a stand against the Indians. It was an old Apache stronghold and, all along the way, McGrew pointed out the places where different people had been killed. Pinal itself had been an army outpost and, from the towering summit of Picket Post, soldiers had watched the plains below, flashing the news to Tucson with their heliographs whenever they saw Indians on a raid.

To get rid of these troops the Tonto Apaches called all their warriors together, lighting hundreds of fires along the summit of a cliff that overlooked the Post. But the bold Captain did not wait for the Indians to attack. As soon as night fell he rode forth with all his men and at dawn they jumped the Tonto camp. A few fought back, but most of them leaped over the brink to their death on the rocks below, for which the cliff is called Apache Leap.

After the Indians were wiped out, the Silver King mine was discovered, and for years a great mill thundered away at Pinal, as it pounded out the rich ore. Then the price of silver went down, mine and mill were closed, and the inhabitants moved away. When we pulled into the abandoned town a single man remained — Fatty Perkins — McGrew's partner in the cattle business and commonly known as the Mayor of Pinal. He lived in the old bank and corralled his horses within the walls of the dance hall. In the gulch behind his residence there was a pile of champagne bottles big enough to fill a saloon, and the beer bottles were beyond all count.

Without doubt Pinal had been a live town while it lasted, but in the seventeen years since the boom had busted, McGrew had hauled most of it away. First the doors and windows, then the timbers of the mill, the stamps, the shafting and the belts; until now empty houses stood sightless, gazing out through dismantled window-holes where the stone walls were falling away. A man who owned a brick house in Pinal was surprised to find it standing in Mexicantown, Tempe, some eighty miles away. Mike had needed a return load after hauling in supplies and he had torn it down, a wall at a time, and sold it to the storekeeper. It was a hard country, all right, and Fatty Perkins earned his living by just staying there.

Just for that he could brand two hundred calves a year, the increase of some four hundred cows, and the cowboys would do all the work. Perkins cooked for the round-up and fed them well — and the first four came up early to catch some wild cattle on Apache Leap. These outlaws had escaped the general round-up for years, until now they were wild as deer. And whenever a valley steer wandered up on the peaks they taught him their fear of man. They were led by Old Grandpaw, an enormous bull; and Daisy, the grandmother of the herd, had lured many a cow away.

Ott Porter had bought the remnant of several old brands; and Johnny, Phil and Worth had irons of their own. The cattle belonged to anyone who could catch them; but it was to prevent the rest from going back to nature that they rode forth into the wilds. It is a dangerous business, running down wild cattle, and above Apache Leap the country is so rough that even the outlaws shunned it. All except Old Grandpaw and his band of renegade followers — and the boys were out to catch them or kill them.

First Johnny rode off over the mesa to the valley which his mare, Mag, used. It took half a day to get a rope on her and the other half to shoe her front feet. It took another half day for four men to shoe her hind feet, and cinch a packsaddle on her back so it would stay. Then, tied to the tail of a soberer horse and with a heavy pack to break her spirit, Johnny's Mag decided to trail along and they set out for Apache Leap.

One week later Mag walked thoughtfully into Pinal with three hides and some loose skillets on her back — but the smell of the fresh hides and the rattle of the hardware no longer had power to disturb her. There was yelling and riding going on up the valley where, in the gathering darkness, four worn and gaunted men were bringing in the rest. Twenty-three sore-footed cattle — and Grandpaw.

UPPER—   McGREW, THE FREIGHTER,
    on his long grind up the canyon to Pinal.

LOWER—   OTT PORTER,
    the horse-hunter who caught old Grandpaw.

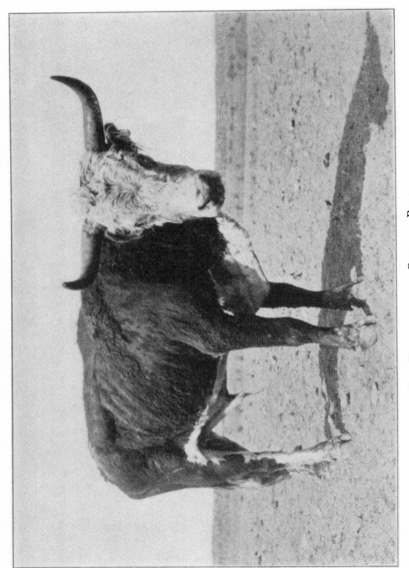

OLD GRANDPAW THE OUTLAW BULL.

He crippled along in the van, still looking for a chance to escape, his horns and hoofs festooned with the ropes of his captivity, a gunnysack hung over one eye. Behind followed a bunch of sore-footed cows and calves, all marked by the rope and iron. One of the boys was sick, another had burned his fingers to the bone on a rope; and, behind them all, limped Porter's pet horse, holding his swollen foreleg above the rocky trail with agony in his eyes. Porter had poulticed the wound with cactus pulp and driven him twenty miles. It was pretty rough going for a horse on three legs, but Ott said three was better than two.

The fire in Perkins' fireplace burned blue that night, being built of planks from the old mill which were strongly impregnated with quicksilver, and it added a sense of unreality to the tale of the Apache Leap drive. For six days the boys had ridden the spiny ridges, holding their captives in a box canyon by building a wall across it and sleeping beside it at night. Their horses had lived on grain and a little browse, *they* had lived on bacon and bread, and each day at dawn they had begun a desperate chase which ended only with the light.

Riding out together they would cut the trail of some band of cattle, following it until they broke cover. Then, each singling out his prey, they would gallop after them over the mountains. On the second day they had discovered the main herd and, while one followed old Daisy and the others picked cows they knew, Porter took after Grandpaw, the bull. It was a mile before he saw more than the end of his tail as it snapped over the top of some ridge. Then the heat of the day and the friction of the rough rocks began to tell on his feet.

There was a smell on the wind like a blacksmith shop when a hot shoe is placed against a hoof, and as Porter spurred nearer he could see smoke trailing out behind. The bull's feet were burning up from running over the lava and he slowed down almost to a walk, but a cow pony knows his business as well as a man and Porter's horse leaped over the boulders like a spike buck. The way to catch a critter is to catch him quick, before he gets his second breath. The bull heard the clatter of iron-shod feet behind him and turned to get away. There was a rush over the rocks, a slash of the rope and Porter's horse sat back on its haunches.

Like a wild animal Porter swarmed off and ran down his rope, and when the bull reached the end of it he felt his head twitched back under him and went tumbling among the rocks. Then the cowboy was upon him, plunging a violent knee into his flank, jerking up his hind feet, and tying them before he could kick. There was a swift uncoiling of hogging-strings, he noosed the bull's forefeet and pulled them back with a jerk. All four feet were drawn together and he was hog-tied — but not beaten. Would he ever submit to being

22

driven to the valley? Porter doubted it, but he had to try.

Johnny, Phil and Worth, now miles away, each had his own problem to solve. Johnny had roped old Daisy, and a steer, and left them securely tied. Phil had tackled a mean one, that scrambled to its feet the moment it hit the ground and came charging up the rope. There was nothing for Phil to do but turn him loose and "git" — and his horse was in on that, too. But when the steer stopped and raced away over the rocks the pony was hot on his trail.

Phil swung down and picked up the rope on the run, and this time the steer landed with a thump, breaking its neck in the fall. Here was bad luck for Phil, for the animal bore Johnny's brand and with a whole neck would be worth thirty dollars. But he stripped off its hide while the carcass was warm and packed the quarters back to camp.

Spurring and humping through the brush, Worth and his mountain-bred horse took after an amazing big steer. He was red, and a fighter — likely to kill you if he got the chance. Worth had tied to cow-brutes like that before and lost his rope — been glad to do it, in fact. This time he crowded him close, waited till they came to an open place, threw for his hind legs, and missed. The steer bounded on, Worth's rope caught on a stub; and there he was, hung up.

But the old burnt-hoof smell still came down the breeze, they followed it for a mile, and there was the red-eyed steer, changing his weight from foot to foot and trying to do all his sweating through his nose. If wild cattle could sweat all over, like a horse, and get off of the lava rocks, the boys would have to go after them with rifles and bring them back as jerked beef. Worth and his horse knew that the steer was tired and they rushed him again, but missed. A third time — and the mountain-bred horse was dead-beat. Crazed with fear the steer ran on for miles, until his hoofs were burnt black and he was hopelessly stampeded. Thirty dollars worth of beef, capering off into the wilderness.

So passed a half day on the heights behind Apache Leap, and the other half days were like it, varying in misfortune for horse and man. For this was not a game played by Porter and Johnny, Worth and Phil alone. Each nimble-footed horse had the spirit of a man. He snuffed the wind for cattle, following the tang of smoke with all the fiery ardor of a *vaquero*. And, during the roping, he played the struggling victim with the alertness of his sweating master. Horse and man worked together, and both knew it. So did the steer, and it helped break his spirit.

But do not think that the steer was broken yet. If Johnny had released old Daisy, who had once been his corral cow, and turned her head towards camp she

24

BEHIND APACHE LEAP.

"Zalliwagger", the most Whole-Souled Vaquero in the Bunch.

would have come up that rope with her head down and tried to gore his mount. He left her there for two days and rode away on another fresh trail. Likewise Porter snaked Old Grandpaw off the sharpest rocks and left him double bound. The sun beat down on his head all day and the coyotes watched his struggles by night, but still he was on the prod.

On the third day the boys brought a band of gentle cows to where he lay with his head tied to a stake. Fastening a *reata* to his hind feet, they cast loose the binding ropes and flew to get on their horses. Then they moved the gentle cows closer, Porter slacked the *reata* and the old bull struggled to his feet. But not to limp slowly to the stone corral and get a drink of water.

Up the side of the canyon went Porter, and after him charged the bull. Then Johnny, down below, set up a hectoring yell and the outlaw charged back at him. Having driven them all out of the canyon he returned at last to the gentle herd, and as their calm minds soothed him a little he plodded slowly back with them and got a big drink at the spring.

Leaving him there, with a few cows for company, the boys drove the rest over the ridges and picked up old Daisy and the others. There was nothing to eat in the stone corral, but they had to drive these cattle twenty miles over a trail and they did not want them too strong. It was better to beat them over their tails with the ropes

25

than to fight them among the rocks — and they got some of that, too.

The horses were gaunted for lack of roughness, having eaten no hay for a week, and their ankles were cut by sharp rocks. Porter's mount had pierced his leg to the bone with the spine of a Spanish bayonet, and everybody was tired out. Phil was sick, Johnny had a burned hand and Worth was willing to quit. But the outlaw cattle fought to the end. Then, filing slowly into the corral at Pinal, they gave up and sank down, beaten.

Chapter 2

THE RODEO AT PINAL

THE invincible spirit of horse and man had conquered these mountain outlaws and got them off the range; but there were three thousand more, running wild in the Queen Creek Basin, and the round-up had just begun. They call it *rodéo*, in Spanish, but the cactus cowboys pronounced it rodér. The contest riders of today have given it another twist and call it ró-deo. Ro-dáy-o is right but, whatever you may call it, it is a legal institution in Arizona and its proceedings are governed by law.

No cow can be branded or earmarked except on the *parada*-ground or in the course of a regular rodeo and — though this law is honored more in the breach than the observance — it shows what is going on. There have been more range wars started by the violation of this rule than there are steers on the whole Pinal range; and it is to avoid such trouble more than to coöperate in the round-up that the cowboys come when they are called.

More than twenty men owned the cattle that were running around Pinal. Each animal had a brand on its hip as broad as a ham; with crops, bits and underhacks in its ears galore. Beyond these marks of ownership

27

it was as free as a deer. But, such is the simple nature of cattle, that they "use" in the country where they are born, unless forcibly driven away. The calf runs with its mother and learns her ways. They drink at the same springs and water-holes, and it is upon this home-instinct that the practice of Western cattle-raising rests.

With millions of dollars worth of cattle ranging around over the public domain there must be some restrictions placed on the activities of zealous cowmen. Otherwise we would have a repetition of that Western anomaly, the acquisition of unnumbered cattle from the natural increase of an old ox-team. A man handy with the running-iron would brand more calves, ten to one, than he was possessed of cows. So the owners are mighty particular to be there or send a man to represent them, when the call for a round-up goes out. It is the harvest time of the cattle industry and he wants his calves branded right.

So the rodeo-hands came trailing into Pinal, each man riding a horse and trailing two more behind him, for that is the least it takes. One day out of three is all the riding that a horse on the rodeo can stand. On his gentlest spare-mount the rider had packed his blankets, wrapped in a canvas tarp, a bundle of tobacco and cigarette papers, and perhaps an extra jumper and shirt. The rest of his wardrobe was on him — two pairs

28

of pants, a jumper and a wide sombrero, boots and a pair of shaps.

His saddle had a steel horn that was built to hold a bull, and there was nothing on horse or man that did not serve a purpose. The broad brim of his California-style sombrero shielded his face from the thorns when he slashed through some cat-claw after a steer. The closed, leather leggings protected his legs from the cactus, and his jumper fended off the brush. The heavy Spanish bit guaranteed that his horse would always agree with him, and the spurs would send him through hell.

Even the long *tapaderas* that hung flapping from his stirrups were not without their use, for when a steer charged to gore his horse he could slap them in his face. There was nothing frivolous about him except the leather fringe on his shaps. He was organized for business.

First came Old Man Bellamy — Dad Bellamy, who lived up Queen Creek at the foot of Apache Leap. He brought his baled hay in a wagon and camped within the walls of the store. Then came Stacy Penn, and Charley and Uncle Cy Whitlow. If it had been a meeting of the Sons of the American Revolution you would not have found more aristocratic names. Then came Old Man Arthur, tall and grey-eyed; and "Mexico," Charley Whitlow's older brother who, having once spent a few days in the land of *mañana* and big liars, was never able to speak the truth again.

Then drifted in the Mexican hands, Guilo and Guero, Juan and Conejo, the rabbit; employed by Perkins and McGrew, who could not themselves ride on the round-up. And last, dashing in over the hills from Tucson, came Josefo, nicknamed Zalliwagger, the most whole-souled *vaquero* in the bunch. He came to serve his master, a German merchant in the Old Pueblo, but he rode and roped with a wild joy all his own.

Out in the open street — and away from the ruins where no scorpions or centipedes would move in on them—the boys threw down their canvas-covered beds and lay where they could hear their horses. The Mayor of Pinal, commonly addressed as Fatty, spread a long table in his house, and there the hands were fed on bacon, beans and bread, canned vegetables and triple-extract of coffee.

After supper that night they gathered at the wagons to help McGrew unload the last of his hay, and then there was a long pause.

"Well," spoke up a voice from the darkness, "who's going to be boss this trip?"

Everybody knew, for it had all been decided in advance, but the form of an election had to be gone through with. At every round-up a rodeo boss is elected, who decides where they shall ride each day and where they shall hold up the cattle. He must know every canyon and every cow, every brand and every man; and he must be able to guess what iron each *orejano* or maverick calf ought to wear in order to satisfy the rest. When you undertake to determine the parentage of an orphan calf you are setting up to be a little Solomon, so there is not much electioneering for the job.

After complimentary nominations of all the older men, Dad Bellamy himself spoke up.

"Boys," he said, "I don't know any man who knows this country better than Stace Penn."

Stace had been the boss the year before so, after the proper protestations, he said:

"I haven't ridden the range much this year, boys. The best man for boss is Dad Bellamy. What do you say?"

"That's right," agreed the cowboys — as if there had been any doubt about it — and Dad was declared elected.

"Is there any man here," he began, "who wants to work Bronco Mesa? No? Well, what about Brush Canyon?"

No one was stuck on Brush Canyon.

"Well then, if it seems reasonable to you —" the rodeo boss is always polite about it — "we'll go up Queen Creek in the morning and make the *parada* at

Arnett's ranch. I want every man ready at four o'clock, and we ought to be on top of the ridge by sunrise."

In the cold darkness of three A. M. the boys crawled out of their blankets and stumped around feeding their horses. Then, all atremble with the cold — for in Arizona a summer's night is not a summer's day — they sat down at the table and ate all they were going to get until the sun rose and set again — very little, in fact — and drank their bitter coffee in silence.

Out into the night they hurried again, and soon each man was riding to his post on the top of Queen Creek ridge. When the sun rose there was a cowboy on every peak, watching the cows as they went down to drink. Fifteen rocky canyons debouched into the big one, and down each ridge or wash a cow-trail led to the water. Cattle are like deer — they feed at night, drink at dawn and bed down during the heat of the day — and the general plan is to catch them while they are drinking and start them down the main canyon. After that they are held up on the *parada*-ground, where the calves are branded like their mothers and the steers cut into the town herd.

Wild cattle are like deer in another respect. When they hear someone coming they will sneak into the brush and hide instead of stampeding down the canyon, and the boys like to get the jump on them. So the waiting cowboys let out a few yells and started down

A Break for the Hills.

The Rodeo at Pinal.

the trail towards the water. But there is something devilish about certain steers — they will not even drive downhill. Stacy Penn rode up on one of these outlaws and had to tie him down and leave him, to be reclaimed in due season by a bunch of valley cows and escorted to a place in the beef herd.

If the boys let these mean steers get away the whole band will turn mean, for a herd of cattle is as wild as its wildest member. Once in the early days a herd of seven hundred was made so crazy by one ornery old stray that, where before the cowboys had ridden among them and counted their calves like rabbits, all they would hear would be the crash of their retreat as they ran off through the brush. So they caught the old cow with a Winchester rifle and raked the whole range clean.

Down at the mouth of Queen Creek canyon, on a level piece of ground, three horsemen who had completed their circle stood waiting the approach of the herd. It is easier to drive wild steers down the canyon than it is to stop them on the *parada*-ground; and as a lure — to check their flight and keep from getting gored — they held a band of tame cattle in front of them.

Cow after cow came shambling down the wash and sifted into the herd. Then came a big steer, with spreading horns and a lithesome swing. He had not seen a man in a year, and despised them all. Shaking his head he charged straight through, but half an hour later he was stretched out in a distant canyon, with all four feet tied together and a barley sack over his eyes. He went into the beef herd, too.

Now came the main tide of cattle, romping along down the canyon, but they stopped short when they saw the hold-up herd before them, the old cows bellowing for their calves. They had been rounded up before and knew what it meant. But the mean ones threw up their tails and charged, and there was some fierce yelling and riding.

While some held the herd, Johnny and Phil and Worth and Zalliwagger struck out over the mesa to turn back these flying animals. Where they could not turn them they roped them; and if they missed they kept right on until help came and the brute was thrown. "Never quit" is the motto of the *vaquero*, and the old cows had come to know it.

The bawling herd was moved out to the middle of the cutting ground, where the riders would have plenty of swing-room, and while half of them held the cattle, the others went for a drink of water. It had taken half a day to gather the herd and, without waiting for further refreshments, the work of the afternoon began. Dad Bellamy, Zalliwagger and Charley Whitlow took off their shaps, lit a mesquite-wood fire

34

and got out the branding irons. Phil and Worth rode
out among the cattle and spotted the mothers of the
calves. Guilo and Stacy and Johnny hovered between
the herd and the fire, to rope them by the hind feet
when they passed; and as the first calf went by, dragged along by the neck, Stacy threw his loop in front
of him. He twitched it up as the little calf stepped
past, but the noose did not snare its wobbly legs. Then
Guilo jumped in and made his cast, the upper edge of
the loop curling over so it could not escape again. He
jerked the *reata* taut, turned without looking back,
and the calf was stretched out by the legs.

Phil called out the brand and earmarks of the mother,
Zalliwagger grabbed the calf; and, while Charley
Whitlow cut crops and bits in its ears, Dad took a hot
iron from the fire and burned a Circle Heart on its
hip. The rope around its neck was thrown loose and
the little calf ran back to its mother, standing and
trembling while she licked the blood from its ears.

— Meanwhile there was another scuffle. Worth had
roped a lusty calf and was dragging it toward the fire
when Zalliwagger rushed forth with the joyous caper-
ings of a small boy. He seized the calf by the tail and
with a great heave jerked it down. Then, as the calf
gave vent to loud bawls, he clapped his hand over its
mouth, imparting a ludicrous quaver to its cry — all in
the most benign manner imaginable. It is a curious

thing about cowboys that they never seem to associate pain with the use of their knives and hot irons; and, since the work must be done, why not have a few range jokes?

No sooner was this calf branded and thrown loose than another victim was dragged up. He was due to have a large pair of scissors burnt on his hip, but there was no Scissors stamp-iron on the fire. Here was where Dad Bellamy displayed the high art of the profession. Hooking a red-hot iron ring from the fire he thrust two sticks through it from opposite sides and held it fast. Then with the hot edge he traced a pair of scissors that covered the whole hind-quarter of the calf.

This process is known as "running a brand" and, while wholly admirable as an art, it is regarded as a bad sign for a cowboy to be too good at it. The Cattlemen's Association of Arizona has placed several such range artists behind the bars for altering other people's brands, and already there was evidence that another brand-burner was in our midst. Some reprobate had been changing Fatty Perkins' FP to a dextrously executed Skew G, and Dad aimed to make this Scissors brand large and inclusive.

He was doing fine when there was a yell from the direction of the herd and two wild steers came thundering towards the fire. Zalliwagger and Dad dropped calf and running-ring and made a run for their horses,

36

UPPER—
 "Zalliwagger", jerked the calf flat.

LOWER—
 Dad Bellamy, running the scissors brand.

Two Wild Steers came thundering Towards Them.

Worth + Frank

just as the steers rushed by them. In a cloud of dust we could see Phil and Johnny trying to turn them away from the brush, but they went into the mesquite with a crash of dead limbs and everyone took to horse.

From the thorny mesquite trees came the "Hya-a! Hya-a!" of the pursuers, the scrabble of hoofs over stones; and at last the two steers came smoking back, heads up and tails popping as they raced each other for the herd. They had had enough and were humping themselves to get to the protection of their fellows; but another wild one had broken out below, and after him flew Zalliwagger and Phil. When they headed him he dodged, when they cornered him he charged. But, as he passed, Zalliwagger's rope settled over his horns, his horse hunched and the steer threw a somersault.

Other ropes noosed its legs and it was helpless. Then Zalliwagger laid a loop over the steer's hind feet, the other boys cast loose their ropes and, swinging its head towards the *parada*-ground, Josefo turned it loose. The steer rose to its feet, looked them over defiantly and started once more for the hills. So they busted him and left him tied, to think it over for a while.

Back at the cutting-ground the boys flew at their work, for the sun was getting low and the beef steers were yet to be cut. All calves with their mothers having been properly branded there was a caucus over the *orejanos,* or orphaned calves, that went something like this:

"Where'd this calf come from?"

Someone said they had jumped him at the head of Wood canyon with two FP cows and their calves, and the rodeo boss spoke again.

"Looks like he might belong to old Funny-face. Believe I saw her with this calf before she died. Does anybody claim it?"

The Mayor of Pinal waited for any rival claim to be made, then he said it was his and the brand was duly made. Every man in the outfit had known old Funny-face and recognized her markings on the calf, and so on with all the rest. On a small round-up like this, where everybody was on the square, the mavericks were identified by common knowledge and branded by mutual consent.

But not all the cowmen at Pinal were honest and, after the beef critters had been cut out and the herd turned loose, Phil put his rope on an old cow and the hands gathered to examine her brand. Everybody knew the animal — she was Phil's old corral cow — and after combing back the hair Phil said a few things about the Sprat outfit that would not look well in print. Her brand had been burned over to the awkward Skew G — and it was not the only one, either.

Here it was again, cattle rustlers on their range, and

38

while they drove the beef herd back to Pinal the older men talked it over. Fatty Perkins had been taking life too easy and he was shy forty calves already, but that was not legal evidence. This altered brand was, and they put the old cow in the corral. But it is the hardest thing in the world to make a charge of cow-stealing stick. Somebody else might have burned that brand to get the Sprat brothers into trouble, and as they were known to be a fighting outfit it was decided to wait a few days.

The Mayor of Pinal was in a terrible fix, for he had a few neighbors who were not above killing him if he cast any aspersions on their character; and on the other hand he was losing cattle, as the records of the round-up clearly showed. But a few days later a message came from the sheriff that more than a hundred FP calves had been sold to the butcher at Globe. He was therefore summoned to identify the hides and swear out warrants for the Sprat boys' arrest.

Those who have ever lived in a cattle country will know how Fatty Perkins felt, but the old-timers made up his mind for him. With Old Man Arthur he started for Globe that same night, and the cowmen hung their guns on their saddles. The next day two long-haired men with heavy six-shooters hanging at their hips came down to the *parada*-grounds and helped in the branding of the calves. They were artists with the running-iron, but it was noticed they kept close together and wore their guns the whole afternoon. They were the Sprat boys, come to look the outfit over and see if Perkins was gone, and they had a surprise coming to them.

That evening three men with high-powered rifles and a hunting look in their eyes, came riding over the trail from Globe and stopped for the night at Pinal. They were members of the newly organized Arizona Rangers, and they had come to get the Sprat boys. But they did not want them right away. So they waited till morning, making a few pointed inquiries, and the Sprats acknowledged their guilt by flight.

So far so good, but there was another bad man who had not heard the news. They kicked in his door at daylight and scared him so badly that his jaw fell down and stayed down. He had sworn he would never be took, but when he saw the muzzles of those high-powered rifles he changed his mind right then. Then two Rangers took after the Sprat boys and caught them before they got to the Line. They were bound over to appear in Court for stealing Fatty Perkins' calves, but jumped their bail and escaped into Mexico.

The Rangers were glad of it, for it taught their friends not to bail out professional cow-thieves. The other bad man was convicted and, with the Sprats out of the country, the men of Pinal were well pleased. If

JOSEFO TURNS IT LOOSE.

One of the Sprat Boys — with a Pistol on his Hip.

one or more of them had been convicted the others would have sworn vengeance and they would have had another range war. It was indeed a happy day when the Sprat boys took to the brush, and all the Pinaleros hoped was that Mexico was large enough to hold them.

Chapter 3

ALL CRAZY

THE NEXT morning the town herd drifted off down the road and I found myself alone in Pinal. It would take every cowboy they had to get that band of outlaws to Tempe, and when Perkins discovered that I was going to stay he suddenly decided to go. It was not every day that he could find a man who was willing to hold down the town, but the coming of the rodeo hands had broken in upon my Nature photography, which prospered best unobserved.

While I was waiting for the round-up to begin I had caught three rattlesnakes and some other reptiles, but before I got around to pose and photograph them, Uncle Cy Whitlow rode in and deprived me of my specimens. It was the first morning of the rodeo and, while I was over the hill getting pictures, Uncle Cy, being of an inquisitive nature, had visited the abandoned mill where my reptiles were hung in sacks against the wall.

Fatty Perkins had objected so violently to my keeping them in his house that I had been compelled to remove them to the mill, where I could hang them out of reach. But Cy, while prowling around, had spied these mysterious sacks and, being quite deaf as well as born with deformed arms, he had failed to hear the snakes rattle until, climbing up on a box, he had reached up with his short arm and felt of them. When he realized what it was he was playing with he had grabbed up a long iron pipe and battered them to a pulp.

There were dents in the plastered wall an inch deep where he had swung on them with his midget hands and when I came back from the round-up I had a hunch that something was wrong. His eyes were burning like lanterns and, all the time I was there, he never spoke to me. Perkins was nearly as bad and I was glad to get rid of them while I photographed in peace. The only companion I had was a little yellow cat, which was in constant fear of its life on account of a big coyote.

On the second morning I was roused up at dawn by the savage yappings of this creature and when Kitty came in through the open window I picked up Perkin's shotgun, which was loaded with buckshot, and laid the coyote out cold. After that the little cat followed me everywhere and slept on my bed at night. I never realized how hazardous life could be for a cat until, three days later, a crazy Mormon drove in and his dog broke my kitten's leg.

This dog was a huge mastiff, which rushed out at me every time I passed until he was finally tied up by his master, who kept a shotgun between his knees and never said a word. He camped out in the open, sitting all day in his buckboard without even watering his horse. It was tied to the wheel in the broiling sun and, for lack of a drink, refused to eat what little hay it had. Every evening I had to go past these miserable creatures, all three of which were going mad, in order to wash my photographic plates in the creek, and it took all the nerve I had to go down after dark and bring them back.

In the rocks along the creek there were tree toads which kept up an unearthly din, and I never knew when the dog or the man might make an attack on me. The cat, with his leg tied up in a splint, took refuge on my cot, and every day two or three hobo miners would limp by on the trail to Globe. It was twenty miles either way to the first food and water, and for years Fatty had found himself burdened with the duty of feeding every man that passed. They were all broke and all starving and, when he went on a strike, the first miners that passed had knocked the bottom out of his water bucket and thrown it down the well. In a desert like that there was no law above that of necessity, and if you didn't feed a man he was likely to take the food anyway. He would be a fool to starve.

After a week of feeding these hobos I developed a new-found respect for Fatty, although he had not

44

come home as he had promised. But with the Sprat brothers at large and these hobos on the trail I didn't blame him a bit. I had become almost as scary as the cat, jumping at every sound; and when a couple of heavily armed men drove in, I kept my eye on them.

They were travelling in a hurry in a buckboard, but after I had cooked up some of Perkins' provisions for them, taking the starvation edge off their appetites, they became almost human.

"Ever hear of Mammoth Tank?" the talkative one asked and I told him it was right up the trail. Then he loosened up and told me his story. The man didn't live who could carry such a secret in his breast; and, while he was talking, the crazy Mormon hitched up and went away. Things were getting too spooky for him.

The secret, of course, was about a hidden treasure, and all the time they were telling it they kept looking down the road, as if expecting a stampede of men. An old prospector, crazy with the heat, had been brought into the hospital at Phoenix and in his mutterings had talked of nothing but gold. Gold and Mammoth Tank! These men had been the first to hear about him and see the chunk of gold tied up in his shirt-tail, and they had been travelling day and night to get there first. But as they talked the matter over they realized the flaw in their tip. There were about forty Mammoth

45

Tanks, all over Arizona, and the question was — which one? Which hole in the rocks was full of gold, and where were the rest of the stampeders whom they had so confidently expected on their trail?

They cooled down by degrees as they sat out on the front porch at Pinal and waited for the rush which did not come, and finally the talkative one was reminded of another rush he had led. This was up north, near Bill Williams' Mountain, and with his pardner he had come to a deserted mine where the water in the spring was alum. It had tied his pardner's stomach into a hard knot and, unless they found some sweet water, it looked as if he would die.

The mine was down in a canyon between two rocky ridges, and everything was in as perfect condition as if it had been occupied yesterday. There was a deep shaft out on the flat not far from the alum spring and, when his pardner had been taken sick, he had moved him into a good house. Then he had hobbled out their horses, which seemed to be scared about something — and pretty soon he was scared, too.

Strange sounds, like the mewing of a cat, came from just outside the door and as he looked out he saw the shadow of a man. Yet when he stepped to the door, the shadow was gone. He walked around the house without seeing anyone, but when he got back to the door, he found his pardner had fainted away. And in

46

the dust there was the imprint of huge, bare feet, going into the house and coming out again. This gave him such a scare that he drew his pistol; but when the man stuck his head around the corner, he was too surprised to shoot.

He was perfectly naked, with a great shock of yellow hair, and his entire body was covered with a thick fuzz or fell, from living in the open sun. He was a wild man, gone back to nature, and there was a sly look in his eyes. A dangerous look, too, and when his pardner recovered from his faint he said the man had tried to kill him. That night the terrible creature hung around the house, mewing and scratching at the walls, and as he was evidently insane the prospector decided to kill him. Otherwise he could not leave his pardner alone — and without water the sick man would die.

But about midnight the wild man disappeared and the next morning the prospector, taking his rifle with him, started out on the trail of the horses, which he felt sure were heading for water. Over the summit of the western ridge he found them standing by a spring and, with a canteenful of water, he was riding for home when he came across another mine. An old Irishman was "herding" it, to keep jumpers away, and when the prospector asked about the wild man the Irishman told him to look out.

He was a young miner whose head had been injured by a fall, and the Irishman had been so terrorized by his mewings at night that he had tried several times to shoot him. But before it became light enough to see his sights, the wild man went away. He lived on cactus pears and any food he could steal, and every time the herder came back from town he found his house broken into. When he heard about the sick man, left alone at the other mine, he told the prospector to get back there as quick as God would let him. Galloping down the trail he came out where he could look down into the valley; and there, standing at gaze, he saw the wild man looking at the house.

He would walk closer, and stop; and when the prospector charged down on him, instead of running away, he headed straight for the door. It was still a distance of several hundred yards but the prospector jumped off his horse, drew a bead on him, and knocked him over the first shot. When he got back to the house his pardner had fainted again, but a taste of the sweet water soon brought him to.

Before the prospector left he had given his pistol to his pardner and told him to shoot on sight, and that gun had saved his life. The wild man had rushed in to kill him and, after firing one shot, the sick man had fainted away; but the shot had scared off his enemy until his pardner returned with his rifle. Just before

48

they left, the prospector dragged the body to the mining shaft and threw it down the hole and, twenty years later, there was great excitement when somebody discovered the bones.

After telling me a few more like this, my prospectors whipped off up the road, leaving me with something to think about when I woke up in the watches of the night. The next morning my poor little cat was gone, and he never came back. He must have ventured out during the night and some coyote had snapped him up.

It was a dangerous country for man or beast, and everybody seemed to be crazy. When we had stopped at Whitlow's Well on the way up the old Dutchman who was in charge there had made himself very disagreeable. McGrew had dragged in some heavy mesquite logs to add to the Dutchman's woodpile and all the thanks he got was the remark:

"Well, it's better than a kick behind."

But there was a heavy sandstorm on, which made it necessary to move into the old house to cook, and while we were eating our supper, the Dutchman began on his pet phobia by asking what we thought of J. P. Morgan. As McGrew declined to be drawn in on the argument I took up the cudgels for millionaires in general and J. P. Morgan in particular; but when the Dutchman went away, too mad to talk, McGrew warned me to lay off, which I did. The next morning as we pulled up the canyon the freighter told me just how crazy he was.

The Dutchman, of course, had a mine which he valued at millions of dollars and when a prospector came by he had inducted him into a partnership, as he was afraid to go underground. The prospector was to go down the shaft and do the digging, for which he was to receive half the gold, but the first time he went down the Dutchman dumped the windlass on top of him and left him there to die. After waiting for two days for someone to come and rescue him, the miner began to dig footholds up the walls and, being blessed with unusually long legs, he had finally straddled the shaft and worked his way to the top. But, instead of having it out with the treacherous Dutchman, he was so glad to escape with his life that he took off across the desert without even stopping for a drink.

But the Dutchman was not the only crazy man at Whitlow's Well, as I found out when McGrew came back. An engineer who was tending the boiler for a well-borer had stampeded their cattle on the way out and the boys were hunting cows yet. Some of the wild ones that they had brought down off Apache Leap had headed back for their mountain fastnesses and never would be caught.

50

ALL CRAZY

In order to hold their herd on the long drive to town the cattlemen of Pinal had built a huge corral out of boulders which had stood for several years. It was all of eight feet high and built accordingly. The herd was safely inside when — at five o'clock, his quitting time — the engineer reached up and blew the whistle. That was a sound never heard before by this band of outlaw cattle and they laid one wall of the stone corral flat as they hit it in a body and left there. McGrew had been camped under a palo verde while he cooked up a little grub and the next thing he knew he was up in the top of a tree. It happened as quick as that.

Well, the engineer said he had always blown his whistle at quitting time, and he didn't know the cattle would run. The cowboys had all said that the corral would hold *any* herd, but in this it seems they were mistaken.

They jumped their horses and turned back most of the cattle, but in the night the herd stampeded again — and in fact, every night, till they got to town. It was a fitting end to that mad phantasy of roping and riding — the rodeo at Pinal.

Chapter 4

THE FOUR PEAKS ROUND-UP

THE SALT RIVER VALLEY was still green and fertile when I went on my next rodeo; but the wide, sandy flats along that once-turbulent stream were growing up to cottonwood and water-moodies. They had had another drouth and the water was still low, but out on the desert there was grass. Six-weeks grass and desert wheat — poppies, Indian paintbrushes and forget-me-nots. Everything was very beautiful, but beginning to dry up. You could see it already, although the cat-claws were bursting into bloom and the hillsides were painted with gold.

It was the spring of 1904 and Johnny Jones was my guide. He had been raised on drouths and sheeped out for ten years, but he was as laughing and gay as ever — until we came to a sheep camp. The grass had disappeared, and now the ground was tramped flat. It was March and they were shearing, before they crossed the river and started north. We came upon them suddenly in a collection of movable corrals, where, never looking up, the shearers were blading away with their perpetual, back-breaking stoop.

Everybody was busy and we rode by without stopping, but out where a buyer was weighing huge sacks

JOHNNY JONES.

AN OLD-FASHIONED PASTOR, OR MEXICAN SHEEPHERDER.
A peaceful, pastoral individual, pathetically eager to talk.

of wool, a sheepman looked up and hollered. I didn't know him for one then, but later learned to recognize them on sight. He was gaunt and tired-looking, with a month's growth of beard and a slightly saturnine smile; and for a rich man he was very poorly dressed. But a worker, you could see that; and he greeted Johnny like a friend. Johnny greeted him like a friend, declining an invitation to dinner; but after we had ridden past, I found out they were far from friends.

Ten years before, Johnny's father, Dr. W. W. Jones, had run cattle on this same range. Thousands and thousands of head, from the crossing of Salt River south. Then, in the middle of a great drouth, the sheep had come in on him and fed the grass down to the rocks. They had taken all the desert, and the range along the Verde; and now, with a mere remnant of their former herd, Johnny was fighting to hold his upper range. His father had died, he had his mother and four sisters to provide for; and unless he was polite to these sheepmen they would exercise their constitutional rights and sheep him off the public domain.

The smile on Johnny's lips would have done credit to Judas Iscariot, but when we got away from there he called down a curse on all sheepmen that sounded like a prayer. I had always thought of sheepherders as a peaceful, pastoral people, pathetically eager to talk to somebody, glad to have even a yellow dog for

53

a friend. But before I got through going to the Salt River round-ups I saw a new kind of sheepman.

The modern, fighting sheepman is as different from the old-time sheepherder as a wolf is from a rabbit. He is a big businessman, playing a game for big stakes against every adverse condition. He goes armed, and his herders go armed; and he used to make a hundred per cent on his money, every year he brought his sheep through alive. And then, when a drouth came and the feed got short, there was a battle for the range that always ended the same. The cattleman lost and the sheepman won. I know of only one cowman who ever beat the sheep and he had to turn sheepman to do it.

The upper range of the Four Peaks is tucked in between the peaks and the box canyon of Salt River, where not even a mountain sheep could cross; and there was a deadline along the ridge west of Cottonwood Canyon which the cattlemen were trying to hold. But any lawyer will tell you that a deadline is illegal, and the mere name makes a sheepman wild. As a matter of principle he will fight his way across it, and Johnny Jones and the rest of the Salt River cowmen had never found an easy way of turning them back.

Every cattleman in Arizona has been up against the sheep and lost, but this was thirty-four years ago and they still had hopes. The big hope of the Four Peaks cowboys was in a Forest Reserve, designed to protect the watershed of Salt River and keep erosion from filling up the dams. Roosevelt Dam was only twenty miles up the river from the mouth of Cottonwood Canyon, and it was hoped that the Forest would be proclaimed before the sheep came in.

We stopped that night at the ranch of Johnny's uncle, Pancho Monroy, an old-time Mexican cowman from Caborca, Sonora, who had been there for thirty years. He had fought off the Apaches and held his own against drouths and disasters; but, being within a few miles of the Salt River Crossing, the sheep had fed him out. Ninety thousand head went through twice a year, from their winter range on the desert to their summer range in the White Mountains; and all the stock he had left was a little band of goats. They could rear up on their hind legs and feed on browse which the sheep could not reach, and the old man was content.

He ran a bunch of cattle on the Indian Reservation a few miles up the Verde River, raised a little corn when it rained and lived the life of a country gentleman. Day or night, you were always welcome to his house, and no one had ever paid him. But when the sheepmen borrowed his rams to lead their flocks across the river and did not bring them back, he rode after them and tried to collect.

Don Pancho had been mayor-domo on a big estate down in Sonora, having many vaqueros under him;

but when after many years of faithful service his *patron* complained of something he had done, he took it to heart and quit. It was his greatest pleasure to tell the story of his master's beautiful horse and how, when a thief had stolen it, he had called Monroy from the round-up and ordered him to bring the horse back.

For eight months the mayor-domo had followed after the thief, until he crossed the Colorado river and went down the Coast of Lower California. It took about two hours to tell the tale, which ran on something like this:

"And from La Palmilla to Santa Cruz was ten leagues. The people were very poor and lived on fish."

The exact distance of every day's journey was given, and what the people ate; and when he caught up with the thief at Ensenada and turned him over to the authorities, he gave all the distances going back. He returned in triumph, having done his duty and brought back the master's horse, but when his *patron* reproved him for spending so much time he called for his pay in cattle and drove them to Arizona.

Don Pancho's eyes were blue and his skin was fair, but he claimed he was *puro* Yaqui. What he was in fact was Yaqui Mayo, a descendant of the ship-wrecked Norsemen who landed at the mouth of the Mayo River, hundreds of years before the Spanish came. Whenever on the West Coast you find a blue-

56

A Modern, Fighting Sheepman.

PANCHO MONROY. LOOKING UP SALT RIVER FOR THE SHEEP.

eyed Mexican you can bet you have found a good one; and simple-hearted Don Pancho was *muy hombre,* as they say in Spanish — very much of a man. He had been a great friend of Johnny's father — a Floyd-Jones from Hampton Island, Virginia — but regretted that young Juanito had inherited his father's violent temper, which was always getting him into trouble. It was no use fighting the sheep, he said. They had come down from the north like an adverse force of nature, sweeping everything before them, and it was better for the cattlemen to submit.

The father of Juanito was a brave man, he said, and — after he had let the sheep pass out of pity and they came back and ate him out — he had sworn an oath to kill every sheep and sheepherder that crossed his range. He had met them at the river and turned them all back, but they had gone away around and moved into the country below. And every year they came back, twice as many — for every ewe had had her lamb and many two — and, if he did not let them cross, they stayed and ate off the range. It was better not to fight them.

As for Johnny, he said nothing, more than to help out when I could not get the old man's Spanish; but the next day, when we rode up the river for the rodeo, he pointed out the spot where a sheepherder had been killed the week before. He had been going down to the river to get a drink and must have stumbled over some rocks because his pistol had fallen out of its holster, struck on a boulder and shot him between the eyes. They had found him dead and sent for the coroner; but it certainly was a coincidence, the way that bullet had hit him between the eyes.

The cowboys never carried guns any more — there wasn't a pistol on the whole Four Peaks round-up — but there was a crazy man who lived up on Bulldog Cliff and did all sorts of queer things. We could hear his hounds baying when we went by on the trail and he had a big, high-powered rifle which he fired when people came too close. He had been kicked in the head by a horse and was liable to do anything. But if a cowboy carried a gun it looked like he intended to use it, and some of those big-headed Chihuahua Mexicans might take a shot at him.

Johnny was perfectly frank as to the reason why he left his gun at home. The sheepmen seemed to try to hire herders who had killed people, mostly Mexicans from Chihuahua and Durango who would get their heads blowed off as long as they got the other fellow, but it wasn't that so much. The sheepmen were organized in a powerful association and, if a cowman killed a herder even in self-defense, they would have him hung for it, anyway.

They had a big "defense fund" and, when Zack

58

The Four Peaks Round-Up

Booth killed two herders up on Tonto Creek, the association used it to help prosecute him, and he was hung. Zack was a good man around the prison-farm, too, and the warden had tried to have his sentence commuted to life; but no, the association wanted to make an example out of him, and they had. A few cases like that would cause a cowman to think twice before he picked a fight with some bad Mexican. Johnny hadn't carried a pistol for years — he was afraid he might get mad and use it. So they were kind of sucking the hind teat for a while until they could get the Forest Reserve declared, but they had had a little trouble the year before and of course they might have it again.

It was a very subdued bunch of cowpunchers who gathered at Cottonwood Creek for the round-up, and nobody mentioned sheep. Unless all signs failed another drouth was coming and they decided to rake the range clean of everything old enough to ship. Eem Cole was the boss for the Jack Steward outfit — he spent all his time on the range. Johnny Jones represented his mother and sisters, his father having stipulated in his will that all the calves for the first eight years should be branded over to the girls.

That was the Virginia gentleman's way of providing for his women-folks, but it made it rough for Johnny. Because as the girls grew up they got married and he had a couple of brothers-in-law on his hands, to make sure he didn't rob their wives. Don Pancho, also, kept a fatherly eye on the tally-book to see that the calves were properly branded — two years to the oldest daughter, two more to the next, and now the third girl was getting hers. Meanwhile, Johnny was getting nothing, more than the expenses of running the cattle, but he took it all in good part. He was a Virginia gentleman, too, and recognized his obligations as the surviving male of the family.

On all the upper range there was just one house — a corrugated-iron structure where Eem Cole lived when he was not out riding the range. Eem was a hustler if ever there was one; and he had a big, gray horse named Stranger that would take him over anything. On the back of his favorite mount, Eem looked like a little boy; but when he took out through the brush and cactus you could see he was all man. He and Johnny were great friends, having lived together and turned back more than one herd of sheep, but the rest of the Americans were small cowmen from the north and east, down to see that their calves got branded right.

There were twenty or thirty irons on the Four Peaks range and, on account of fighting off the sheep every year, the percentage of mavericks was high. On the other hand there were several boys who rode with a

On all the Four Peaks Range there was just one House — at Cottonwood.

Jose Maria Roblero, the Top Roper of the Outfit.

telescope in a rawhide case, fastened to the back of the saddle, and that is a very bad sign. The glasses were used to read the earmarks on wild cattle when they stopped on some ridge to look back, and if any yearling had got by the round-up it was more or less the custom of the country to ride after him and correct that oversight. Only instead of giving him the brand of his mother they would slap on one of their own.

While not exactly stealing, this was considered unethical, and it calls for a lot of explaining when the cattle are brought together at the round-up. At the same time, on the circle, when a big *orejano* or eared-one was jumped, half the men on the outfit might take after him and the first man that tied to him lit a fire and branded him, right there. According to law every maverick taken on the round-up is supposed to be branded over to the State Sanitary Board, which looks after the health conditions of neat animals but is concerned principally in stamping out rustling. It inspects all brands, and records all shipments and sales to local butchers, but in those happy days the man that caught a maverick branded him and laughed over it.

Our biggest laugh was on Juanito, as his Mexican *vaqueros* called Johnny. Unlike the hundred-per-cent-a year sheepmen, the cowboys were all dead broke. The only man in the outfit who had a dime was Juanito himself, and he had fifty cents. A lone fifty-cent piece, which he flashed whenever somebody offered to bet him a thousand dollars, and nobody had ever covered it. He kept it in his overalls pocket and when the boys were pitching horseshoes and betting yearling heifers for stakes he pulled it out and fondled it lovingly. But as nobody could bet with him he forgot all about it, and didn't even know it was there.

Now the year before, while Johnny was sleeping on the ground, a hydrophobia skunk had attacked him; but his long curly hair had protected him from its teeth, though the skunk had broken the skin and given him a bad scare. There were a couple of months when he never knew for sure whether he might not wake up biting the door-jamb, and ever since that time he had slept in the wagon-bed for fear another skunk would come around.

On the day of the big laugh Juanito had tied down a maverick calf and was heating his running-iron to brand it when Jose Maria Roblero came around. Jose was a kind of cousin, or some distant relative, and a joker in a shrewd way.

"How much will you take for your calf, Juanito?" he asked.

"Cash?" inquired Johnny. "Fifty cents."

He pulled down his mouth and rolled his eyes roguishly; but Jose Maria reached down into his pocket and brought out a fifty-cent piece.

"Hell!" exclaimed Johnny, jumping up and reaching into his pants; but the half-dollar was gone, had been, for several days; and Roblero, coming across it, had slipped it into his pocket, saying nothing.

"Take the calf!" said Juanito, grabbing the fifty-cent piece. "A man with no more sense than that deserves to lose."

Jose Maria took the hot iron and branded the *orejano*, right there. After that he was always offering to buy something for fifty cents, cash, but Johnny would feel in his pocket before he opened his mouth. This Jose Maria was the top roper in the outfit and, being older than Juanito, who was still just a boy, he rather took charge of the Mexicans. The Americans ate at one fire and the Mexicans at another, as they like different kinds of food; and in the morning, when it came time to get up, Johnny would keep on sleeping. This gave Jose Maria the chance he sought to usurp a little authority and he would begin to holler.

"*Arriba — Juanito!* Up, Johnny!" he would shout. "*Morrales!* Get out your nose bags!"

The horses were turned out hobbled every night, on account of the feed being short, and in the morning they would go out to catch them with a nose-bag half full of grain. But Johnny would grunt and groan and cover up his face with his tarp until his officious cousin would grab him by the leg and get him up for the

63

day. Then he would start a fire and unwrap the beef, which we had shared with our American friends and, while somebody put on the Dutch oven to cook bread, somebody else would start the coffee or mix up some baking-powder biscuits. It was every man for himself, after that, but there was always a pot of beans over the fire, and the Mexicans could about live on beef.

When a critter was killed they would hang it up to cool over night, then cut long thin strips the length of the grain, wrap them with strips of fat on a stick and broil them over the coals. They ate all the tough meat first — only, the way they cooked it, it wasn't tough — and would often let the tenderloin spoil while they were broiling shoulder and plate. After a big feed all around they would wrap the carcass in a tarp and every man, before he rode off, would throw his blankets on top. When, an hour or so before sundown, they unwrapped it to get more beef, the meat was chilled as cold as if it had come out of a refrigerator.

There is no use talking, the Mexicans can tell us a lot when it comes to handling meat. A side of beef would keep four or five days, lying out in the broiling hot sun; and when it began to get a little ripe they would slice all the meat off the bones, rub it with salt and ground chili-peppers and hang it in the sun to dry. A sack of this jerked beef came in very handy when we were moving or out of fresh meat; and they can toast it over the coals, beat it to shreds on a rock and get a meal started in jig-time.

Beans come in handy, too, but are difficult to transport; and bacon is far too expensive for the bean-kettle. They use beef-fat and chili-pepper, and the average Mexican outfit could feed its men on twenty cents a day. The Americans were always cutting tin cans and cooking up big batches of bread; and they were never happy without stewed fruit and canned tomatoes, potatoes and onions and all the rest. It made a lot of work at the end of a long day, but the Mexicans would sit around the fire for an hour, broiling beef and eating it off the stick, and at the end there would be no dishes to wash, except a few that could be scoured in the sand.

It was a little outfit, eight Americans and eight Mexicans, and the country was as rough as Pinal. The last two years had been dry and the cattle were thin but none of them had died on the range. Feed being scarce, the sheep were crowding in on them; and when, in the spring, they nipped off the tender grass, no more grew. Cactus the sheepmen were shy of, as its stickers became imbedded in the wool and hurt the shearers' hands; but the Four Peaks boys were expecting them any time and they worked the upper range first.

A spell of hot weather had melted the snow in the White Mountains and kept the Salt River up; but sheep were coming across it, down at the upper ford, and the cowboys flew at their work. The cows all had calves, but that kept them thin, and they wanted to get the beef herd across the lower range before the feed was gone. From Cottonwood, the end of the wagon-road from town, we moved by pack-outfit to Cane Spring, then on to Asher's Basin, where Henry Brown held forth.

Henry was an eccentric, to say the least, and he had lived there alone so long he had almost forgotten how to talk. He never shipped out his cattle — except a few, to buy some grub — and all he wanted was to be left alone. He lived under the overhang of a sand-stone cliff and spent most of his time smoking cigar-ettes, but when the round-up got to Cane Spring he always came over to help. So the boys rode in and helped him work his stock. Sometimes they would find cows five years old and still unbranded, but he knew them all by sight and only branded the calves.

Henry had queer ideas about Government and had refused to pay his taxes from the first. When the Gila County tax collector came around he would say: "My cattle run in Maricopa County." And when the Maricopa collector sent in a deputy he told him they ran in Gila County. Jeff Adams, the Maricopa Sheriff, finally came over and seized a hundred and fifty head, but that was long afterwards and it almost led to a killing.

The Four Peaks Round-Up

Brown was lying in wait for the officers at the western entrance when, taking advantage of the low water in Salt River, they crossed from the southern side and drove off enough cattle to pay his taxes for forty years.

He was a Texan and on the prod like a wolf, but with our boys he was very friendly and he sent out quite a bunch of stuff. It was a good thing he did, too, because a few weeks later the sheep moved in on him and fed his grass down to the rocks. His range lay in a basin, surrounded by high cliffs — a kind of pocket, tucked in between the river and the ridge. No one ever dreamed that the sheepmen could get into it, or that they would have the nerve to try; but they had ninety thousand sheep to feed and the weather was getting dry.

We moved back to Cottonwood in a hurry and the sheep were clear up to the deadline, as the cowmen had expected. Lucky they hadn't crossed. It was on their regular trail and they were drifting north a mile or two a day, feeding off the last of the grass that had sprung up since the rain. Their comings and goings were nicely timed to take full advantage of the seasons. Now that the winter rain had brought up the grass they were moving to their northern ranges; and, after a summer in the cool pastures of the White Mountains, they would come back in October, to feed off the range again after the summer rains. The rest of the time the cattlemen could have it and welcome.

Arizona Cowboys

One after the other the big sheep-owners came through and made some jesting remark about the grass, but the cowmen were all too polite to even mention the deadline. They were on their good behavior, after a run-in the year before when a herder had been thoroughly worked over. Not a cowboy was armed, but the herders all had rifles, and as a couple of fighting Mexicans crossed the ridge I rode up to take some pictures. It looked as if they were coming over, and that afternoon the boys stayed in camp; but they changed their minds for some reason and the sheep were driven back. Then Jim Swope, the owner, rode down and had a little talk with Johnny Jones.

He asked if they still thought a deadline was legal, or if they could turn back his sheep if it was; and that night somebody had a hunch. Whoever it was, this cowman took some boiled beans and soaked them in a can of strychnine. Then he climbed up the ridge and dropped one here and there, where the leaders would pick them up if they came. His hunch was correct for, early in the morning, the first wave of sheep swept over the divide, headed for the upper range.

Some were in favor of riding up to meet them, but that had been tried before. Everything had been tried — and the memory of Zack Booth, hung by the neck for killing two sheepherders, lay over the cow-camp like a pall. It was hard to think of what that range would look like after ninety thousand sheep had been over it — and if the first herd was allowed to pass the rest would follow, that was a cinch. They were still talking it over when Jim Swope on his black mule came galloping along the ridge. The leading sheep had stopped — some had lain down — and, after turning the rest back, he headed for our camp.

"You so-and-so," he yelled, addressing Johnny. "What the hell do you mean, poisoning my sheep?"

"W'y, you must be crazy," answered Johnny. "I don't know what you're talking about."

"Yes you do!" charged Swope. "Them sheep has et strychnine. They was eight of 'em dead when I came by there and —"

"Well, don't talk to *me!*" came back Johnny. "I told you yesterday not to cross that deadline, and if you'd listened to reason and stayed where you belong, this trouble would never have happened. But say — you keep your hand off that pistol or I'll take it away from you and beat you over the head with it."

Johnny was beginning to go out of his head a little, and Swope put up his gun. But he was mad — mad all over — and as he rode away he shouted back dire threats.

"Let the Mormon-faced bastard talk," said Juanito; and the next day Jim Swope was gone. But the day after that there were sheep all over the range. The upper range, which Johnny thought he was protecting, and as the cowboys spread out over the hills they discovered that the sheepmen had fooled them again. While Swope was making a bluff to cross their deadline and keeping them all in camp, the sheep had crossed Salt River up above and moved in on Henry Brown. They were coming out the entrance of Asher's Basin, one band after the other, and before they got through with that upper range they made the cowboys look sick.

But just when they were having a big laugh, somebody began shooting up their camps with a high-powered rifle. The bullets came from so far that no one could hear the shots, but most of them fell very close. One herder reported later that a bullet had pierced his frying-pan while he was eating out of it by the fire. Where the sheep were bunched up they made an easy mark, and whoever was doing the shooting was a dead shot. More than one herder fled, leaving his flock to the coyotes, and everybody blamed Henry Brown. But anybody can shoot up a sheep-camp, and some of the cattlemen had gone wild.

It was almost a war while it lasted and when it was over the rodeo had been broken up and the upper range swept clean. The cowmen had lost, as usual, and in the next six months they had a drouth on their hands.

Chapter 5

THE DROUTH

IT WAS a drouth which brought the first predatory sheep into Arizona — the Drouth of '76, which drove the Daggs brothers and their sheep out of California. That was the worst dry year in the history of the State and, knowing that their sheep would die anyway, they struck out east across the Mojave Desert, hoping to get some of them to the grassy mesas of northern Arizona.

But, instead of losing their sheep, they encountered galleta grass and other feed clear across the desert and brought them to The Needles in good condition. Since sheep can live a month without water in cold weather they were especially adapted for the trip and when they came to the Colorado River the Daggs boys learned something more about sheep. Having no money to pay the ferry they forced their herds into the river, and crossed them without losing a sheep.

The Daggs brothers left their herds in northern Arizona, which later became a sheepman's paradise, and went back to California for more. This is spoken of as the beginning of the sheep industry in Arizona — although the Navajo Indians had long before brought in herds from New Mexico—and for many years afterwards the Daggs family were the biggest sheep-owners

71

in Arizona. They understood the business and their legal rights, and when the drouth of 1891-2 came on, finding their range fed out, they pushed their herds south until they crossed the Salt River.

It was these sheep which had come down the Verde River and moved in on Dr. Jones and, out on the desert below Florence, they opened up a winter range which they have occupied ever since. Here, in a climate where frost is almost unknown, they fatten their wethers on the rich desert grass and tend their ewes through lambing time. It is another sheepman's paradise, where they can shear their sheep in February, and in a short time the town of Mesa became their headquarters in the south.

In the north they held forth around St. Johns, in Apache County, where the genius of Sol Barth had reconciled two warring factions of colonists by dividing the town in half. On one side of the main street the Mexicans made their homes, and on the other side the Mormons, and those are the two elements most commonly represented in the Arizona sheep business. In fact, they got together and fought off the Texas cattlemen who had settled on the plains around Holbrook, until the cowboys had to admit they were whipped.

Then the New Mexico sheepmen bid themselves in on this sheep-and-cattle war — and let no man say the

THE DROUTH

New Mexicans are not fighters. For two hundred years their ancestors had been standing off the Apaches until they had bred up a strain of Spanish Americans that would rather fight than eat. If it was trouble the Texans were looking for, they could get it any time when they tackled a Chaves or a Baca. But the Mexicans who were carrying the guns in the Four Peaks country were another breed entirely.

They were the same mountain outlaws who, a few years later, got behind Pancho Villa and Orozco and overran all Mexico. They were fighters, too, but of a baser sort; and, except for the war-chest of the sheep-owners, the cowboys would have run them off the range. It was not the fighting that the cattlemen were afraid of, but being brought into court in some county dominated by sheepmen and sent to the penitentiary for life — or hung, like Zack Booth. So, in this last bout before the drouth, not a sheepherder was killed; and, when they left, the upper range was cleaned. To be sure Henry Brown, or some other cowman, had shot up a few Mexican sheep-camps; but the only thing that worried the sheep-owners was having their sheep killed off.

When the bullets began to fly and their herds were stampeded they moved them, and moved them quick. Two thousand head of sheep were worth ten thousand dollars — you could hire a herder for forty a month.

73

In Wyoming and the states to the north a good sheep-herder drew seventy-five dollars a month. Twice as much as a cowboy — hence their cynical saying that a cowboy was a sheepherder with his brains knocked out. But the social status of the cowboy was immeasurably higher. The sheepherder was a social outcast.

The cowboy rode a horse — the mark for thousands of years of the *caballero*, or gentleman—and the herder walked, like a peon. But give that peon a pistol and a 30-30 rifle and mark the sudden change! Pancho Villa did that, only a few years later, and he found they would stand up to machine guns. The sheep-owners hired these Old Mexico *pelados*, fed them well and went with them, and they would cross any deadline in the world. Some of them were like small boys who had been given their first gun. The height of their ambition was to kill somebody.

That was why the Four Peaks cowboys had left their guns at home, but it would never happen again. When Johnny Jones came back from taking in the town-herd he had his six-shooter in his bed. Not on his hip, where it might attract attention, but hid where he could get it quick. It was a little late, of course, since the sheep had all gone north and a drouth was coming on; but they would be back, he knew that. Whether it rained or not, they would be right on his neck and he could make up his mind all over again,

74

A Chihuahua Mexican with his 30—30.

A dangerous combination, as Pancho Villa demonstrated a few years later. In the background, Weaver's Needle and Superstition Mountain.

UPPER—
    American cowboys, talking it over.

LOWER—
        Over the rocks and cactus.

whether to shoot some poor ignorant *pelado*, hired for forty dollars a month, or let the owners take the range.

Some of these owners were old friends of his — or claimed to be. He had known them since they were boys, gone to school with some of them; but when their sheep invaded his range, these friends were conspicuous by their absence. They would send their herders in and tell them to sheep him out, then go off to some sheepmens' convention and come back to see what had happened. Once, when one of them met him later, he patted him on the back and said:

"Well, Johnny, I knew you were going to be sheeped out, anyway, and I thought you'd rather be sheeped out by a friend than by someone who wouldn't treat you so well."

When Juanito started cursing he had some terrible names for these friends, but sooner or later he would remember his duty and try to pull his face straight, and smile. When his father had died he had told Johnny what he expected of him, and it did not include getting killed in some quarrel with a Mexican sheepherder. It was his job to hold the cattle together and give each of the girls two years' calves. But his youngest sister would not get very many, with this dry year coming on; and Johnny could see it was dry.

I went to town with the beef herd and didn't get

back for two years, but he gave me all the details of the drouth and had some more names for his "friends."

When he got back to Monroy's ranch, his uncle was out cutting brush, and he had a story a mile long to tell about the *año seco* that was even then upon them. All the world was drying up. In Hermosillo and Caborca, Sonora, the women stood in line all night with their ollas, waiting to dip a little water from the wells. Even now their cattle were dying along the river, too weak to stagger back to the distant hills where the sheep had left a little feed. But if he would go out with his axe and cut down the short-leaved palo verde trees, they would browse on the tops and perhaps that would keep them alive.

That set Johnny to thinking, though he made no promises — for a cowboy hates any kind of work that can't be done on a horse. But, back on the range, he found the cattle eating cactus and gnawing at the coffee-berry stumps. Everybody said the cattle were not dying, only a few, but as he rode back to his camp at the mouth of Cottonwood Canyon he counted the carcasses along the way. The next day he went up to Hidden Water, the only unfailing water on the range, and he found more dead ones there. They would come down and drink a big bellyfull, then lie down to rest, get cramps in their legs and stay there till they died.

He hated to do it, but he had to get out the axe.

The Drouth

While he was cutting the first tree, an old water-bum cow stood watching him, and when the top hit the ground she tottered over and began eating on it. Six or eight other cows that were hanging around joined in and fed it off, and when he chopped down another some old outlaws that had been watching from the ridge forgot their fears and horned in. By the end of the week he had a hundred and twenty head that followed him wherever he went.

Up at Jack Steward's headquarters, three men were sinking a well, so the cattle wouldn't have to walk so far. They would come down from the upper country with their bellies full of cactus and bitter brush and drink until they could hardy stand; but if they ever lay down they could not get up. One old cow seemed to know that, for she leaned against the cliff for two hours, then started back on the range. Some went as much as eight miles over the ridges before they could even find browse, and practically all the calves were gone. The mothers could hardly rustle for themselves and had no milk for their little ones.

One day while he was going to work Johnny heard a cow low and found a little spotted runt which had fallen through the limbs of a palo verde tree and couldn't get up. He brought her a couple of buckets of water and that evening he got her out. The next day he gave her a flake of baled hay and she headed back over the range, but three days later he heard her low again and found her wedged in between two rocks. After he had helped her out and fed her again she followed him like a dog.

When short-leaved palo verdes became scarce Johnny piled a lot of brush around some fuzzy chollas and tried to burn off the thorns, but the fine stickers got into the cows' tongues, which swelled up until they couldn't eat, and they died in two or three days. So he went back to cutting palo verdes, no matter whether the thorns were long or short, and every morning as he went out to work he was followed by a string of cattle. There were more than he could feed, but as he was hacking his way in to a tree he felled an enormous giant cactus, which burst open when it landed in the wash. A short time later, when he looked down, he found the cattle gathered around it eating out the pulpy inside.

After that he went along the sides of the canyon, felling *sahuaros* down the slope, and the cows quit the palo verdes entirely. The great fleshy columns would break wide open when they fell and the cattle would rush in to eat out their bitter hearts. The flesh has an odor not unlike a turnip and melon combined, and before the drouth was over thousands of fat desert giants, each a ton or more in weight, lay prostrate in the dust. But, though every day the white thunder-caps rose

78

higher, piling up against the peaks, and the summer heat grew terrible, it did not rain a drop.

The rainy season had almost passed and the water lay in pools along the dried-up river when a change came over the sky. There was a haze that softened the edges of the hills, and the dry wind died away. A sultry heaviness made the cowboys drip sweat as they worked; and at night they could see the heat lightning, playing along the northern horizon. It was a sign of the summer rains, but all they got was the heat.

For a week the clouds piled up against the peaks, and one day they covered half the sky until they cut off the sun. A moist wind sprang up, blowing into the storm's black heart, and the heat was suffocating; but as evening came on the clouds melted suddenly and the sun went down in a clear sky. Johnny had called down a curse on everything and fallen into an uneasy sleep when he felt a drop of rain in his face. He roused up and looked around — the night was black and close, but there was a wind in the trees and as he held out his hand he felt rain. It came in great, warm drops, striking up the dust like smoke, but the earth had forgotten how to drink. Its bone-dry soil set like cement, turning the dust-holes into pools, and before the water could sink in it was gliding swiftly away. Then it lashed down savagely, drowning him out of his bed, but he just stood and let it rain.

It looked pretty good after two years of drouth, and when it rained it rained plenty. Before morning he could hear a roar down by the creek and at daylight Cottonwash Wash was a river, and still the rain sluiced down. Where the water belched out from Hidden Water canyon it formed a barricade that blocked the bigger stream, and when that dam broke it rushed down and stopped the main river, so that Salt River became a lake. Every little gulch was bringing down its quota of brush and giant cactus skeletons; and the trunks of tall cottonwoods, killed by the drouth, went bobbing along with the rest.

The grinding of the boulders in the creek-bed could be heard above the roar of the water, and they smashed down the mesquite trees as they passed. Where Cottonwood Creek emptied its burden into Salt River it dammed the main stream all day, creating a great lake which went out with a crash in the night. Everything was swept clean and, after the storm was over, there was nothing to show for this great glut of waters but the high ricks of driftwood along the banks. That and the sun-dried skeletons of cattle, light as cork, bobbing off down the river in a mad race to the sea.

Chapter 6

MOVING THE SHEEP

THE STORM had ended as suddenly as it had begun and when the sun came out the cattle drifted in to be fed. They had taken to the high ground and escaped the flood, and Johnny went out and cut down a few more *sahuaros;* but on the third day the brittle sprouts of the stick-cactus came out and the cows wandered back into the hills. In a week there were flowers on the bushes and all the flats were green, but the whole country was crisscrossed with a thousand gullies, where the soil had been washed away.

They were just that much nearer to the primeval granite, and Juanito blamed it on the sheep. He said that the flood waters, which always before had spread out and been absorbed by the thirsty ground, had been carried off so rapidly by the sheep-trails that they had washed the top soil away. Cattle, when they feed, spread out in family groups; but the sheep fall in behind each other, and the herders keep them bunched up. Certain it is that, two years later, a large part of the range was still bare; and the trenches, then just started, had widened and deepened, cutting their way to the solid rock.

Johnny was especially bitter against the sheepmen

for feeding off his upper range, just when he needed it most to carry his cows through the drouth. It was the walking back and forth, from water to feed, which had worn out and killed the stock; and he claimed that, if he had been able to protect the grass, he wouldn't have lost ten head where he had lost a thousand. But never for a minute did he fool himself into thinking that the sheepmen would show him any mercy. Rain had followed rain, there was good grass on the flats — but the war between the sheep and cattle would never cease until the last cow was dead or standing behind a barbed-wire fence.

The only hope of the cattlemen was the new movement for conservation which had been started by Chief Forester Pinchot and was being vigorously supported by Theodore Roosevelt. The Roosevelt Dam, up Salt River a few miles, was already beginning to impound water, but a few more such devastating floods as this last one would fill it up with soil. The diversion dams down the river would soon be silted up, too; and the winter before the Salt River watershed had all but been set aside as a National Forest.

But a powerful lobby had come into existence which was opposed, not only to more Forest Reserves, but to any changes in the law regulating grazing on the public domain. It was composed of factions formerly antagonistic, joined together for self-defense — sheepmen and big cattlemen, railroad and lumber interests. And, by alliances with other anti-administration forces, they had the whole conservation movement stopped.

For years the cowman had dreamed of a day when Forest Rangers would draw two-mile circles around their ranches and keep the sheep away. They were willing to lease the land, which they had formerly occupied for nothing, or pay grazing fees — anything for protection. But in this battle for the grass the sheep had come out winners and, from their profits of a hundred per cent a year, they could well afford to contribute to a defense fund.

It was well known that Gifford Pinchot was opposed to the grazing of sheep on the National Forest. He contended that their presence was destructive to the grass; and, if any more Forest Reserves were proclaimed, it would naturally bar that many more sheep. So the sheepmen were up in arms and, while this legislative fight was going on, it was necessary to consider the matter of legal precedent.

By invading the upper range at the beginning of the drouth the sheepmen had established a previous use, which would have to be considered in case it was proclaimed a Reserve. If they could occupy it again it would give them a stronger claim — but the cattlemen were determined to keep them out. Over half their herds had perished, and they had lost their entire calf-

83

crop. *All* the calves were dead, there was no branding to be done — and the rounding up of beef stuff could wait. The big thing right now was to stand off the sheep, and they began to ride the range by days' works.

They were a hard-looking outfit, after chopping brush all summer and dragging dead cows away from the water, and most of them were carrying their saddle-guns, with a new kind of defense in mind. Henry Brown had not been as crazy as he seemed at the time — he had smoked the sheepherders out of Asher Basin without seeing the inside of a jail. In fact, Henry was still hiding out in the hills somewhere and, if any more camps were shot up, it would naturally be blamed on him. So why not run a few more herders out of the country by the system which he had demonstrated?

It was unlawful, of course, but Henry had found the owners' weak spot. They were not in the sheep industry to satisfy any great moral urge nor to demonstrate their rights as free-born American citizens. It was that hundred per cent a year they were after, and when they began to suffer a loss they would move their sheep and move them quick.

The sheep came south in orderly battalions, herd after herd until there were ten in sight, and the leader of the first band was tough. He had killed three men and didn't care who knew it. Incidentally he was the boss herder for Johnny Jones' "friend," who had sheeped him out during the drouth. Johnny rode out to meet him with Bernard and Howard Hughes, two cowboys on whom he could depend.

"Where are you going?" he asked.

"To the Rio Salagua," answered the herder, "to meet my *patron*."

"No you're not," said Johnny. "You only think so. You're going to turn off right here and go out through that pass."

He pointed to a canyon that led off to the west, and the herder reached for his gun.

"I'd like to see you make me," he said.

"All right," replied Juanito and, turning to his friends, he asked them if they were game.

"Just try us," they said; and Johnny did.

"O. K.," he nodded. "You pack up this *hombre's* burros. Don't hurt anything, but pack them up. I'll drive the sheep, myself."

"No, I'll drive them," spoke up the herder; and he put them over the divide. When the other herders saw his dust they turned their sheep out, too, and so the whole outfit went around. There was good feed everywhere — it was the principle of the thing which had prompted his so-called friend to sheep him out. But when it came right to it, that herder didn't want to kill an unarmed man. There might be legal complications which the defense fund could not square. So the first

85

ten bands went out by the lower crossing and the cow-boys still patrolled the range.

Always before the sheepmen could locate them by following the course of the round-up. Now the im-poverished cowmen didn't have any round-up, and they didn't have much to lose. They had been waiting long enough for the Government to help them — to declare the range a National Forest and have a little law — and they were going ahead without any law. They sent a man up north to follow the rest of the sheep down, and patrolled the range on three sides.

From the rim of the Mogollons down the Tonto it was easy to follow the sheep. They could do that by their dust. There were more sheep than ever, for they had come through the drouth in good shape, and the cattlemen along the trail were trying to keep them off their range. But the sheep had to eat, there was no grass along the beaten road, and as they spread out up the hillsides they were mowing the feed down like a mechanism. Like a great machine, that doubled its size every year; and as the cowmen got tough the sheepmen got tougher, though on neither side was any-body killed.

It was up on the Tonto that Zack Booth had shot his two sheepherders, and that made them all a little care-ful — the herders not to get shot and the cowmen not to get hung. So they took it out in hard words, and in

86

the end the cattlemen let them go through. It was the only way to get rid of them. At the least interference the sheep owners would halt their herds and begin elaborate parleys until, crazy with rage, the cowmen would motion them on. For, backed up behind them, were sheep and more sheep, all trampling down the grass, feeding off the browse and polluting the water of the streams.

I have talked with big sheep-owners who assured me positively that the fattest cattle in Arizona were found where sheep and cows ran together on the same range. But how long those cattle remained fat and how long they shared the range, was something we did not go into. A sheepman will tell you that their herds do not pollute the streams, that it is all a bugaboo to say that cattle will not drink after them — and this is probably true. After seeing them eating cactus I can readily believe that to them a little sheep-taste in the waterhole is just one thing more.

There has been a lot of language expended in arguing the right and wrong of the sheep question; but, as a congressman once remarked, that has all been ironed out now.

"Yes," observed a cattleman with a cynical smile. "But he didn't say what kind of irons were used."

The answer is, of course, shooting-irons. Some of the outfightingest men in the West have been sheepmen, and there was one in Arizona who had them all buffaloed. He rode a big, black mule, wore a big black hat and carried a 45-90 rifle; and when, in a hostile country, he saw a cowboy he just stepped off and went to shooting. But he did get quite a set-back when, during the Pleasant Valley War, he brought ten thousand head of sheep into that country.

The Grahams and the Tewkesburys were fighting out their feud in what had always been a cattle country, but they laid off of each other long enough to shoot up those sheep and run Black Hat off the range. And, unless they have gone in recently, there have never been any sheep in Pleasant Valley since. But when Black Hat came down through the Four Peaks country the cowmen danced to his music. Here is the way Johnny Jones described a visit.

"This man Black Hat was sure bad. He had killed ten or eleven men and when I heard he was on our range I left my gun at home. But I went up to see him, all the same, because he was eating out all the feed.

"Good morning," I said. "Are you the owner of these sheep?"

"You bet I am," he says, pulling his gun around in front, "and if it's trouble you're looking for, here's as far as you'll have to go. My name is Black Hat, if you want to know, and any cowman that's looking for trouble gets accommodated."

Moving The Sheep

"Well, hell's bells!" exclaimed Johnny. "If that's the way you're going to talk I'm going to leave here, right now. You don't need to go crazy, when a man asks you a civil question."

"That's the way I talk to them all," said Black Hat. "I don't let no cowman run it over *me*."

"Well," says Johnny, "I'm no cowman, so put up your gun. Can't you see that I'm not armed? I'm just the cook for the Jones outfit. There's ten of them and I'm the only one in the bunch that isn't hung down with shooting-irons. They've gone around the other side of the mountain with the wagon, and they sent me up the river to give you this message. But if you're going to leave the earth the first word I say, I'll let you find it out, yourself."

He got up to go but Black Hat beckoned him back with his six-shooter.

"Here, young man," he hollered. "Come back here. What's this message?"

"Well, since you inquire, it's just this: 'Move or we'll move ye.'"

"Ahhr!" laughed Black Hat. "That's what they all say. But they'll find me right here, when they come."

"All right," answered Johnny. "I'm only the cook. But if you'll take advice from a cook I advise you to move. The feed is good everywhere, and there's no use staying here and getting into trouble when there's lots of grass right across the river. They're sore as hell, and they say they're going to jump you, so look out."

"To hell with 'em," said Black Hat. "Tell 'em that."

After delivering his imaginary message Johnny, who was the whole Jones outfit, rode back to Monroy's ranch and down to the valley, at Tempe. A couple of days later a Mexican came by and told him that Black Hat had moved. He probably got to thinking it over and, as nobody jumped him, moved on to where they *would* fight. This is quite a contrast to the heroic cowboy of Western fiction, who blasts the sheepmen off the range with a six-gun, but for the last thirty years it has been about like that.

The Four Peaks cowboy who had ridden north to follow the rest of the sheep down, heard enough grief to pack hell a mile, and in the general scuffle over the range he was able to twig the big play, when they turned off for the upper range. A few years before, the sheepmen had cut a way through between two of the Four Peaks and now, while the cattlemen were being kept busy on the trail, Jim Swope sent his fighting Mexican to invade the cowmen's stronghold.

It was not that they needed the grass now; but, to a hundred thousand sheep that had come through in the spring, there had been added many more — the she-lambs that were left after shipping the wethers — and the next spring there would be more yet. And all these sheep had to be fed. So they sent this Juan Alvarez to break his way through and put up a fight for the range.

It was a rough place, that crotch between the Peaks, and Alvarez cut his way through chaparral that stood horse-high before he won the southern slope. There the ground was bare and rocky, broken by innumerable ravines which came together in a round valley, then plunged into the defile of a box canyon. This was the middle fork, down which Alvarez would have to come, and the cowmen got together and decided to wreck him, using the sheepmen's own weapons, strategy and guile.

On the high mesa behind the Peaks there ran a herd of forty or fifty wild horses; and, far below, where the valley opened up above the defile, a band of their own horses was feeding. These were all branded stock and, when they wanted to catch one, the cowboys generally held them up in this same round valley. It was a natural hold-up — they talked of building a horse-trap there and catching the wild bunch — but so far they had been content to let them go through. Now they looked down from the high ridges and watched Alvarez as he walked into their trap.

But Mr. Alvarez was too smart to bunch his sheep in the round valley. He drifted them up on the mountainside, where he could look out the country while they fed.

"I'll fix you," promised Juanito; and that afternoon while the Mexican stood guard he saw, far to the west, four horsemen, riding slowly towards him. Instantly he whistled to his herders, waving his arms and pointing, and they moved the sheep out of sight. Down the hill and into the round valley — just where the cowboys wanted them. They passed by far to the south but, as the sheep were now making a great clamor, Alvarez drove them into the box-canyon, where they would bed down and go to sleep. Many years in the sheep business had taught him, into what small compass a band of sheep can be packed, and as the cowmen rode past he kept them there, hid.

An hour later the four horsemen appeared on the mountainside, rounding up their band of tame horses, chasing back and forth to head them off, edging them down to hold up the wild ones. Then as the *remuda* quieted down they rode in on them, swinging their ropes as if to catch some while they waited for the grand stampede. It came just at sundown, a rumble of hoofs from the north where the wild bunch was being brought down.

Down the middle of the broad valley they came on the dead run until, spying the hold-up herd, they swerved and slackened their pace. But, as the cowboys closed in from behind and others showed themselves on both sides, the wild bunch rushed straight for the

A Day's Gather on the Four Peaks Round-Up.

THE WILD BUNCH RIDES IN.

box canyon, where Alvarez was holding his sheep. Catching the contagion of their flight, the tame horses charged after them — and a minute later there were no sheep.

Those that were not down were running like the wind. They were scattered in every direction as they came out of the mouth of the canyon, and the cowboys spurred through after them. Johnny Jones came last of all, looking around for the herders, and he saw Alvarez clinging to the rocks, his eyes as big as an owl's.

"Well!" he exclaimed. "*I* didn't know you were here!"

And Juan, being badly rattled, said something about that being all right.

"But," added Johnny, "it wouldn't have made any difference if I had."

He looked the herders over and laughed as he spurred away out of range, and that was the first intimation they had that someone was playing a trick. They were clinging to the sides of the canyon like bats and, with that many armed cowboys lingering around, they didn't try to round up their sheep. It was three days before the owners heard about it; and, when the news broke, all the other herders packed up their burros and moved. Orders or no orders, they left there; and, having the range to themselves, the cowmen got busy and rounded up a good-sized town herd.

Chapter 7

JOHNNY JONES

THAT WAS the last thing the Four Peaks cowboys had thought of — having a round-up. They had been fighting the drouth and the sheep so long they hardly knew what they were, wood-choppers or gunmen. They had spent more time moving sheepherders than they had branding calves in the corrals, but now they expected a change. Jim Swope was shy three thousand head of sheep, valued at fifteen thousand dollars; and that is a lot of money when you earn it the way Jim got his.

But on top of that Theodore Roosevelt outgeneralled the opposing forces and set aside the Salt River watershed as a part of the Tonto National Forest. A bill was passed by both houses, depriving the President of his power to proclaim Forest Reserves. But, before it became a law, it had to be signed by him. In order to make him sign they held up the entire appropriation of the Forest Service; and at last, in exchange for that, he agreed to sign the bill. But, having secured his appropriations — and before signing away his rights — he used the power still vested in him to proclaim not only the Tonto National Forest but any others which came to mind.

That was pretty fast work and it threw the preda-

ARIZONA COWBOYS

tory sheepmen into confusion. For thirty years they
had been sheeping off the range and their right had
never been questioned. Legally they still had that
right, but the area over which they could depredate
had been materially reduced. A Sheep Trail two miles
wide was laid out for them, from Salt River to the
Mogollon Rim and, when I came back in 1908, the
Four Peaks cattlemen were jubilant. They had had a
good winter, the price of beef was high and, glory of
glories, a Forest Ranger had been assigned to them, to
keep the sheep on the Trail.

In return for this protection they were required to
pay a grazing fee of thirty-five cents a head for every
animal over six months old — and the taxes were thirty-
five cents more; but in the general rejoicing over getting the Reserve, this increase was hardly mentioned.
Johnny Jones had been fighting sheep for fifteen years
and they had fed his range down to the rocks. Now,
down on the desert, there were more of them than ever
— for the sheep had had a good year, too — but wait
till they put their herds over that two-mile Sheep
Trail, and see how good they looked!

My first welcome when we started for the round-
up was from Pancho Monroy, at his ranch; and all he
could talk about was "Reengers." "Rangers" was
a new word in his vocabulary and he could never get
it quite right, but he had entertained a lot of Forestry

95

men since the Reserve had been proclaimed and held them in the greatest esteem. "El Yeem," the new Ranger, in particular he invested with a power next to God; and Jim was going to protect him, when the sheep came up to cross. He was going to make the *borregueros* stop borrowing his goats to lead their timid sheep across, for they never brought them back; and Jim was counting everybody's stock, keeping a record of all the brands.

That was the way they did things down in Sonora — and they collected a tax down there, too; but thirty-five cents was a great deal to pay on a calf only six months old. Still, that was the law and Jim said it was worth it, to keep the sheep off his range. Pancho was going to bring his cows back from the McDowell Indian Reservation when the grass came up again; and meanwhile he was very happy to have all the Reengers for his friends. Jim could speak Spanish and he always stopped for dinner, and often overnight. No, the Señora never complained about the cooking. It was a pleasure to her to have fine gentlemen seated at her table, to tell her the news from the great, outside world.

I must be sure and see her young giant cactus, which registered by a shrunk-up place near its top the result of the terrible drouth. It had been very bad, and many cattle had died; but his had all come through alive,

THE SENORA'S GIANT CACTUS, RECORDING THE DRY YEARS OF 1903-4.

Placed with a She-Goat at their Birth, the Goat-Dogs live with the Herd and Bring it in at Night.

because he began to cut brush for them while the Americans were just talking about it. But El Yeem said that was very bad for the country, to cut down all those trees. When the great flood had come it had washed away the brush; but Jim was smart, he had seen the stumps. Now, before they could even cut a mesquite tree to mend a weak place in the fence, Jim must first come, with the little hatchet he had, and stamp a Government mark on the log.

Yes, yes; everything was changed since I had been there. The big dam up at Roosevelt was finished and they could shut the whole river off. It had made a great deal of trouble for the colony of beavers which lived across the Salagua. When the water was cut off they had dug a ditch a mile long up the slough, to bring water down to their dam. Then, when even that went dry, they came in the night-time and began a dam across the river itself. The Rio Salagua! But before they got it done someone pulled the gate and the beaver dam was carried away. So they moved up on the Verde, where the water flowed evenly all the time, and joined the other beavers there.

It kept Johnny Jones busy, interpreting for his uncle all the changes that had taken place, and still the half was not told.

When the sheep came up to cross, the Government was going to close all the gates at the dam and let them pass dryshod. Then more Rangers would come — they would ride along the Trail — and any herder who drove his sheep outside would be arrested for spoiling the grass. All had been arranged by his friend, El Yeem, who would see that his goats were not stolen.

And I must see his goat-dogs, that took the flock out every morning and brought them back at night. These dogs had been taken while still blind pups from a mother that lived far away and placed with a she-goat having one kid. And while the kid was sucking at one teat the mother could not help but let down milk at the other; until at last, when the dog-smell had left him, she adopted him for her own. When the pups grew up and their mother would not suckle them, they stole milk from the other goats, and ran down rabbits among the rocks. But when they came to the house he beat them and drove them back and now they thought they were goats.

One time the herd strayed away and was gone for a week; but the dogs stayed with them, fighting off the coyotes, and brought every one of them back. They had also learned to fight the Mexican sheepherders when they tried to steal the rams. They were very low people, these *borregueros*, many of them petty crim-inals and robbers from Old Mexico. In Sonora they would whip such *pelados* from their doors; but the sheepmen made much of them, to get them to stay, for the work was hard and dangerous. And to every one they gave a rifle and a pistol — that made it very bad.

It was a great education to talk with Don Pancho and to hear, in the midst of so many signs and wonders, all the things the Reengers had done. The old man was the oldest resident on the river, having come there when the soldiers were still at Camp McDowell and the Apaches on the warpath. So, while he had never pre-empted his land or attempted to file a homestead, he was given preferred rights over everybody. El Yeem, the Ranger, made much of him; and he was well-known to the officials of the Reclamation Service, who often shared his hospitality.

His wife was the slave to everyone, cooking meals day and night for all the people that passed. But they raised all their own beans and corn, and their store-rooms were full of jerked beef and chilipeppers, and hides to trade in at the store. Some envious Mexicans, hearing of the gold buried beneath their floor, had come one night and tried to rob them. But, having been raised in Sonora where such things were common, the stubborn old couple refused to reveal their treasure, even when put to the torture. It was not until he deposited some of his money in a bank that the old man lost part of his hoard, and he was full of wise sayings about thrift.

99

"A good heart needs a tight hand," was one of his favorite maxims, but he was generous to a fault. Anything that he had, if you praised it he would give it to you, no matter how valuable it was; and the only way to break even was to send him some gift in return. Towards Juanito, his nephew, he was now very approving; and he told me on the q. t. that he had ridden the range after every round-up and never found a calf misbranded. For eight years, working for nothing, Johnny had carried out the terms of the will; and by that time there were few cows left that were young enough to have calves for him. But Juanito had been loyal to his trust, and at last he was truly happy.

On the way up the river he would sing in his big baritone voice the arias from Spanish operas which he had learned in some mysterious way, and one day he told me the reason. During a terrible drought he had gathered seven cows and was driving them to town from McDowell. They were so feverish from the heat and so weak from thirst that they tracked along with their eyes shut, their heads down. But out on the desert a big jackrabbit had made his form under a bush by the side of the trail, and when he jumped up in front of them it stampeded the cattle, so that all but two ran themselves to death. After that he always sang in order to keep the cows awake.

His favorite tune was an old song, sung by a young

man to his girl when they could not go out because of
the rain:

> Somewhere the sun is shining
> There's a rainbow in the sky.
> Hush, then, thy sad repining,
> We'll be happy by and by.

Heard during the drouth, when the cattle were dying
for rain, it had a rather incongruous effect; but the
sentiment was right. Johnny believed in optimism and,
as I got to know him better, I picked up little things
about his past. When his father had died, Johnny was
still a boy of sixteen and he had bought a fancy checked
suit to court a girl he knew. But the income from the
estate, which at first was quite large, had just sufficed
to pay the administrator and was rapidly dwindling
away. So Johnny, remembering an old Spanish saying,
had pulled it on the man of the law.

"You be the heir a while," he suggested, "and let me
be the administrator."

But, being a minor, he was not qualified to handle
the estate, though he had quit school and was handling
the cattle. So, in the absence of the administrator, he
swore he was of age and the court had let it ride. Johnny
had worn out his fancy pants and left the coat in a sheep-
camp rather than go back for it; but the vest he wore

for years, to keep his tobacco in, though it got tight across the chest. It must have brought up memories of gay Mexican *bailes* and pretty girls smiling back at him, but in town he spent his leisure around the pool-halls — he could not afford to dance.

In fact his chief delight seems to have been in breaking up the Mexican dances where in happier days he had flashed his fine new suit. This used to be a favorite diversion in many Western communities; but in Tempe, where he lived, it was special. There were many American cowboys in town at night and, when about so drunk, they would ride past the dances, roping the dogs when they came out and putting on a show.

At the head of a gang of kids, Johnny had tried to break up a *baile* himself, but the Mexicans had set three big dogs on them, then caught them and beat them up. When they got back to town they found a lot of Valley cowboys in the saloon, who jumped their horses and rode out to the dance to put the Mexicanos in their places. Leading the bunch was a cowboy, later luxuriating in the name of Cutthroat Charley, on account of a scar across his throat, and this is how he got it.

Riding out to the dance house, Charley roped at one of the dogs but, being pretty drunk, he caught a big rosebush, instead.

"I've got one!" he yelled, putting spurs to his horse; but when he got to the end of his rope the rosebush

Juanito riding a Wild Bull, just for Hell.
He still wears the fancy vest, left over from happier days.

PRETTY WORK WITH THE REATA.
This cow is going to put her hind foot through the loop.

jerked them over backwards. Before Charley could get up the Mexicans came swarming out, and in trying to get away he ran his horse under a clothesline which laid him on his back again. Then the Mexicans jumped him and before he got through with it, he was badly beaten up. The scar across his neck healed up white; and when Johnny came across him on another range he had a desperate story to account for it. But Juanito knew it was not a rustler's loop which had snaked him from the saddle, but the clothesline of a Mexican woman, who took in washing for a living.

Johnny had been around a little, riding for neighboring outfits and getting the run of the country, and one of his first experiences was while working for Jim Bark in the Superstition Mountains, above Pinal. They had killed a beef the day before and he had greased his latigo straps. It was a rough country and full of cactus and the first day out, while riding ahead of the rest, he roped a big steer by the horns. Then his cinch began to slip and the steer, which was going at full speed, dragged the saddle out from under him.

Juanito landed on his head in a patch of chollas, the rope slipped from the steer's horns and his saddle fell on top of him. In order to get rid of it he had to roll over on his back, and when he got out he had spines through his nose and lips clear to the gums, a big joint stuck over one eye and three or four pieces in his hair.

The insides of both arms were full of it, and his back and legs looked like a porcupine's. He had pulled off two or three of the biggest pieces when the whole outfit came by on the circle, but they were all so scared of losing their jobs that not a man would stop.

He hollered, but they kept right on to the *parada*-ground; so he had to saddle his horse, that was as full of spines as he was, and ride half a mile to ask for help. They were holding the herd when he came up, but he finally hired a little Mexican named Mariano, promising to pay him everything if he got fired. It being a hot day in May and Johnny all sweaty from the pain, the cactus came out easy, but it took him two days to get it all. He would pull it out of himself until he cried and then out of his horse until he kicked; and all for a dollar a day.

Every spine of cactus is composed of herringbone barbs, that go in easy and come out hard; and to get out the pieces that were broken off he would rub beef tallow on the place and stroke it with a hot piece of iron. In winter, when the flesh is cold, they soak it out with hot water; but the fuzzy little stickers are the worst. They grow in bunches at the base of the longer spines and, once they get into the flesh, about the only way to get rid of them is to pour on hot mutton tallow, let it get cold and pull it off, thorns and all.

Playful cowboys, when riding by one of these chollas with a tenderfoot, have been known to hook a joint into the fringe of their shaps, then, at the next narrow place in the trail, press it firmly into the newcomer's leg. But this is a very crude joke, as the wounds are very painful. The joints of the tree chollas are so loosely attached that at the least touch they will come off; and it is currently reported, and believed by many people, that they will jump at you as you pass. What happens is that the long, almost invisible spines catch in the clothes, the joint comes loose and sticks; and it takes very careful work, jerking it off with two sticks, to keep from getting thoroughly stuck up.

It takes a certain hardihood in horses and men merely to live in a cactus country and, when they take after some cow over the rocks, two pairs of pants and their leather shaps are not a bit too much. Besides that they generally wear a jumper or two — and the horses are quick as a cat when it comes to avoiding chollas. The ordinary cat claws, mesquites and ironwoods are taken as all in the day's work but when they sight a cactus they will jump high and wide before they will run into it.

The river was high as we rode up it and, when we crossed at Blue Point, our horses almost went down. But by holding them up stream and giving them their heads they managed to keep their footing among the rocks. There were several herds of sheep waiting to cross but, as the water was now controlled at the dam, it came boiling out of the box canyon like a flood. Thousands of acres of land — at Phoenix, Tempe, and Mesa — had recently been put under irrigation, and it was a question whether the Government would cut off the water supply to let a few sheep across.

None had gone over yet and, when we arrived at the mouth of Cottonwood Canyon and found the new grass untrampled, Juanito gave three cheers. Always before, while they were working the upper ground, some adventurous herder would swim his sheep across, and use the big corral there to find out how many he had lost. Then he would feed off the grass that the cattlemen were saving for their horses, and the round-up would get off all wrong.

April first was the date set for starting the rodeo, and also for crossing the first sheep; but when we found El Yeem, the Ranger, he said all that was changed. There was a big demand for water from the irrigation districts below, and the sheep would have to wait. He said the dam had been built to supply the valley with water, not to hold back the river for the sheep; and once more Juanito cheered. It seemed too good to be true, but it showed that Jim was their friend. He had been a cowman himself and knew what it felt like to have his range sheeped out.

Jim was a little slow on his fountain-pen work, and writing out his report was the hardest work he did; but he was determined to keep the sheep on the Trail.

It had been marked by signs on the giant cactus, beginning at the mouth of Cottonwood Canyon and extending to the north — two miles wide, and posted on both sides. All he would have to do was to put them on the Trail and see that they did not stray. And the Jones place was protected, too. There were big signs up in English and Spanish that the corrals were not to be used. They were part of a cattle ranch and the Forest Service would protect them.

Well and good: the cowboys rode into the Jack Steward ranch as if they had come for a picnic. And gathering their cattle would be just that, compared to what it had been before. Jim was right on the spot to supervise everything and keep a record of the calves branded, and not a voice was raised against him, though some of the new rules were onerous.

The next time there was a drouth there would be no cutting of palo verde trees, no busting of giant cactus on the rocks. There was not a live cottonwood left, the whole length of Cottonwood Canyon, and at Cane Spring the canes were all dead. Now the Government had stepped in to halt this destruction, check these man-made drouths, and protect the Salt River watershed. It was part of a big movement all over the United States to conserve our natural resources, but it was for the good of the cattlemen just as much as for the benefit of the water-users. All they had to do was observe the regulations and leave the sheep to Jim.

Jack Steward had a new foreman now in place of Eem Cole — John Gilliland, a cowman of the old school. He had gone through the Pleasant Valley War, being the first man shot in that mountain feud which had bankrupted two counties with its lawsuits, wiped out two families and killed off seventy or eighty men. But he had lived to go back afterwards and round up the Stimson cattle, over which the factions had been fighting, and help restore a degree of peace.

He was a slow-spoken man with a good-natured smile, but Pleasant Valley was right up the Sheep Trail and the herders knew him for a warrior. He had bounced a stone off of a few of them when they came in on him during the drouth, but now he was all for peace. In fact, he left his gun at home when they went out on the first circle, something very unusual for John, and the rodeo was a success from the start.

Among the Americans there were the Hughes Boys, Bernard and Howard; Fred and Charley Cline, Dove and Iva Crabtree, Tim Adams and a cowboy named Stimson. With the Mexicans, Jose Maria Roblero was still the top hand; Mariano Mendibles was there with his fine horses; and the Spanish Jesus Gomez, Johnny's brother-in-law. Added to them were Rafael Velasco, Lopez and Lalo, and a Yaqui Indian horse-breaker named Nacho.

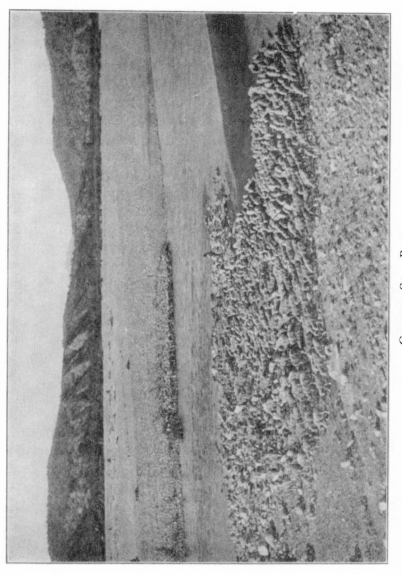

CROSSING SALT RIVER.

The sheep are shoved into the water above a rapid and land on the other side.

Jose Maria, showing the Americans how to Rope.

JOHNNY JONES

A fine bunch of cowboys, and their horses were almost fat enough to pitch. But after a day in the rocks, chasing out wild ones, they were generally too low-spirited for that. The *remuda* was small, not more than three horses to a man and most of them had only two, and they hobbled them out every night. They could graze over more ground that way, for the feed was still short, and every morning at the shout of *Morrales!* they would come hopping back towards camp to get their feed of grain. Rolled barley it was and, with a nose-bag of it waiting, it was easy to bring them in.

The Mexican style on a rodeo is to chase every steer, rope him and tie him. The Americans never tied unless they had to, but would head them off and drive them back. They claimed they could do twice the work in that way, and it was easier on both man and horse. But the Mexicans are all good ropers — it is a sport with them — and in a corral full of cows and calves there would be *reatas* flying in every direction, Jose Maria could rope a cow backwards and pick her up by any foot, so the Americans generally let him do it. If we had a rodeo boss nobody knew who it was, but the work seemed to go on all right.

Most of the cowboys had an iron or two, and Johnny ran ten or twenty brands — holdovers from the days when his father had owned thousands of cattle and was constantly buying more. Dr. Jones was one of the leading men in the Territory and did everything in a big way. He ran freight teams from Prescott, was part owner in the famous Vulture Mine, and made his headquarters at Wickenburg when the Apaches were at their worst. And now, in his own way, Juanito was taking after him, though still on a very small scale.

But when he was riding the range for cattle he was looking for a gold mine to boot — the Lost Dutchman, of course — and always he was thinking *big*. His eight years of servitude had ended and his sisters must have given him back some of their cattle, for they appreciated what he had done for them. Now he was building up a little herd of his own and, at the thought of Jim the Ranger standing off the sheep, he would burst into roundelays. Like his father, he was a wonderful storyteller and everything that came up he got a laugh out of it, somehow.

One day, while the boys were out riding, an American with a brand-new pack outfit came in and began to ask about the Lost Dutchman Mine. That is a favorite form of insanity in Arizona to this day, and Johnny and the rest of them had just about decided it was on the other side of the river. But they had all served their time trying to trail old Jake Miller and locate his fabulous gold mine, and when this stranger came in with his Apache guide I knew what was on his mind.

He did not ask, straight out, for information about

the mine but inquired for mysterious landmarks which would guide him in his quest. So I told him that, being a stranger, I did not know the range; but Johnny Jones knew every canyon in the Four Peaks country and he could ask him when he came in. So, after supper, he came over and began to work his auger on Juanito.

"Mr. Jones," he said, "do you know a hidden spring in this country where the skull of a man was found?"

"Oh yes," smiled Johnny. "It is right down the canyon a few miles. My brother-in-law over here is the one that found the skull."

He pointed to Gomez, sitting over by the fire, and the stranger glanced at his guide. This had evidently been peddled out to him as something extra-special but the first man he asked knew all about it.

"That was the skull of Jerry Miller," went on Johnny, "the Dutchman's nephew, that he killed when he was running away. People claim he did the shooting over at Mormon Flat, but this skull had a bullet-hole right through his forehead and Gomez found it at Hidden Water."

"So!" exclaimed the treasure hunter, raising his eyebrows at his sullen guide. "Oh — do you know a trail this side of the Four Peaks where there is a human face painted on a rock?"

"Sure," returned Johnny. "Been by there, lots of times. It was made by this crazy Mormon that lives down on Bulldog Cliffs. You go right up this second canyon —"

And he described, with great particularity, just how to reach the spot.

"I wonder," said the prospector at last, "if you've ever seen a cave with a big armchair in it, at the base of an overhanging cliff."

"Well," shrugged Johnny, as a crowd gathered round to hear these innermost secrets, "that sounds like this Opeshaw's work. He's the crazy Mormon that lives up Bulldog Canyon. He steals everything he can get his hands on, hides it out in the mountains and then forgets where he put it. Why, he spent months taking his brother's wagon to pieces, packing it up the cliff and putting it together again — away up there on the peaks, where a mountain sheep could hardly navigate. He takes gunny-sacks, clothes, harness, tools —"

"This chair that I speak of," interrupted the stranger, "had a horse's hoof on the right side, where he —"

"Oh! Why didn't you say so?" beamed Johnny. "That belonged to Henry Brown, over in Asher's Basin. He lived in a big cave under the cliff and all he did was sit over the fire and smoke cigarettes until his face was the color of leather. And do you know what that horse's foot was for? He put his cigarette in the frog of it, whenever he wanted to spit."

112

Chapter 8

THE LOST DUTCHMAN MINE

THE STRANGER never knew that Johnny was kidding him, and he went on with such tall stories about the Lost Dutchman Mine that he had us all goggle-eyed. Johnny had spent more time than he liked to admit in the pursuit of this will-o'-the wisp and he was in that low mood when he took a grim pleasure in blasting other people's fond hopes. Every time the prospector asked about some rusty musket, or even about the Dutchman himself, he would lay the goods on the line; and at last he told the whole story.

"This Dutchman," he said, "went by the name of Jake Miller, though some folks said it was Walz. He and his nephew, Jerry, that got killed down the wash here, were Germans that had served in the Confederate Army; but after Lee surrendered they were afraid the Union soldiers would kill them and skipped across the Line into Mexico.

"They came to the big ranch of the Peralta brothers, probably somewhere down in Sonora, and found them assembling about eighty armed peons and a whale of a big pack-train, to boot. That was a long time ago, when Arizona was just a county of New Mexico and nobody lived here anyhow, but these brothers told him this country was full of gold and they were going up to get some.

"When Jake saw some of the rock — which was the pure quill, believe me — he told them they were foolish to take along so many cowardly peons. It would just attract the attention of the Apaches without doing them any real good. But if they would give him half the gold he would go along and protect them, as he and Jerry were both sure shots. Well, the Peralta brothers agreed to leave the peons behind and they came up into this country, going through Tucson and the mountains around Pinal until they got to this gold mine, which was rich.

"They loaded up the mules and went back to their hacienda, giving the Dutchman and Jerry sixty thousand dollars for their half. Then they went up against some big gambling game and in two days' time they were broke. So they came to the Dutchman and asked them to go back to the mine, although they were deathly afraid of the Apaches; and old Jake, taking advantage of their fear, turned around and *bought* the mine. He gave them back the sixty thousand dollars, and all he asked was the use of their pack-train to carry in a lot of supplies.

"Back at the mine they unloaded the mules, dismissed the packers and settled down to dig out the ore, which was easy half gold. But within a month or so Jake and Jerry had a quarrel. Jerry wanted to go to Santa Fe, at that time the Territorial Capitol, and record their claim; but Jake was afraid the Union soldiers would kill them, or start a rush of Northern men that would take the mine away from them.

"But Jerry was bull-headed, and one night he started for Santa Fe. Jake trailed him to Hidden Water and, right there by the spring, he shot him through the head and buried him. Then he went back and kept on digging, but the murder kind of preyed on his mind and when Phoenix was started he finally went down there and hired an old colored woman to take care of him. He sold what gold he had with him to the Valley Bank for $18,800, as you can see by looking at their books, and took in a young Mexican named Rodriguez to help him have a good time.

"This Mexican was a bad one, drunk and gambling all the time, but whenever he ran out of money the Dutchman would bring in more gold. The ore was so rich it got everybody excited and, every time he started out, half the town was trying to trail him. That's why he always came up through this country — on the north side of the river; but when he got up here he lost his trail in the rocks and crossed over down by Mormon Flat.

"In a few days Jake would come in with all the ore he could carry; but one time when he went back he found two soldiers, working his mine. They had been going up over the trail from Fort Huachuca to Camp McDowell and all we know is he killed both of them and buried them near the mine. After that he was afraid to go back any more. He went kind of crazy and, knowing he was going to die, he made a map of the country for Rodriguez.

"Sure, here's where the map comes in — like you read about in all these lost treasure stories; but there's a man named Dick Holmes down in Phoenix that could go right to that mine. He was one of the first to trail old Jake when he would sneak away out of town, and when he heard that the Dutchman was sick and delirious he slipped in and passed himself off for Rodriguez. Well, Jake told him the whole story of the mine, just like I'm telling it to you; but he couldn't give him the map, because Rodriguez had it hid.

"So the old Dutchman died and Dick went to work on the Mexican. Got him drunk and stole the map off him, but after that he was afraid to leave town because he knew Rodriguez would kill him. The Apaches were bad then but Rodriguez made up his mind he would find that mine, anyhow, so he went back to Mexico to hunt up the brothers Peralta, but both of them were dead.

"But there were some old packers who remembered the trail, and they got together about fifty men and led him right to the mine. It had been worked in the old Spanish way, by digging a round hole thirty or forty feet across — and a tunnel, over at one side. They got out enough ore to fill their leather pack-boxes and started on the trail home, but there was a Mojave Apache watching them and he ran back to the Verde, got the rest of the Indians, and they killed every one of those Mexicans — including Rodriguez, of course.

"But here's the joke on the Indians. They didn't know gold when they saw it, so they dumped all that ore in the sand-wash in order to get the leather sacks. It's stray rocks from this float that start all the gold rushes in that big canyon north of Superstition Mountain. There ain't a bit of doubt that mine is up there somewhere, but Dick Holmes has got a *map*. He knows right where it is, but he's afraid to go after it. Afraid my brothers-in-law—or me, maybe— will follow him up and kill him to get the mine. Or the map — it would be just as good.

"I remember a couple of Danes that came down from Colorado to work on the Apache Trail road. They had a map, and explored the country east of Superstition for several years in all their spare time. One of them had a horse he thought a lot of and when a flood came down the canyon, cutting them off from supplies, he went over to the road camp to buy some grain.

"But they were short of feed too and his money was bogus — until at last he pulled out a chunk of gold and left it for security. I was just a boy then but I happened to be over there and I asked one of these Danes if this gold was from the Lost Dutchman mine.

" 'Yes kid,' he says, real sarcastic; and of course that shut me up. Old Arizona Jim is still hunting around for it and claims in a couple of months he's going to find it. He's always inquiring for an old *arrastra* at the head of Pine Canyon, but everybody knows that was built by ore-thieves when they were high-grading the Silver King. But I think, myself, it will be found by some Indian."

Johnny stopped abruptly, lit a cigarette and blew out a cloud of smoke while the stranger waited on his words.

"Why?" he asked at last; and Johnny glanced at the guide.

"Well," he says, "it was the Mojave Apaches and Tontos that killed Rodriguez; and after they robbed the pack-train they went back to the hole to see what the Mexicans were after. They rolled some big boulders into the pit and filled up the tunnel into the hill; and now, of course, they're the only ones that know where the mine used to be. But, not being citizens, of course they can't locate it and the white men would take it away from them; so they're keeping it a secret. I don't know of but one Indian that is game to tell where it is, and unfortunately he is in prison."

THE LOST DUTCHMAN MINE

"What for?" asked the prospector; and Johnny took him into his confidence.

"For cutting his wife's head off," he said. "He made me an offer to take me to the spot if I'd get him a pardon from the Governor. But he's such a bad Indian I can't work it. It seems these Indians have got a superstition against showing any man the mine, and this squaw was going to do that. So he cut off her head to keep her from talking and the Judge sent him up for life."

He rolled his eyes at the stranger and his guide and rose up to go to bed, and the next morning our prospector was gone. He had probably got to thinking what might happen to him if he found the Lost Dutchman Mine. He was on the wrong side of the river anyway, because neither Indians nor Mexicans would venture into that haunted country which lies behind the Superstitions. The story is that a big war-party of Pimas had pursued some raiding Apaches into that country and not one of them had come back. As they could not believe that even the bloodthirsty Apaches could wipe out the whole band, the Pimas had come to the conclusion that some devil ruled over the land. Certain it is that, even to this day, there are prowlers up in those cliffs who waylay and kill intruders; and it is an off year when some hardy prospector fails to find another skeleton with a bullet-hole through the skull.

But the original discoverer of that mine of gold now

known as the Lost Dutchman is believed by many to be Captain Weaver, after whom Weaver's Needle is named. He was stationed at Picket Post, near Pinal, and as the Apaches were wary of the white man's shooting they carefully kept away. Bored at last by the months of idleness Weaver began to ride out with an escort while he explored the surrounding peaks; until at last, venturing out alone, he was taken prisoner by the Indians.

Now it was the custom of the Apaches to torture their captives by all sorts of devices, but so stoical and calm was this white man that they spared him while they thought up something worse. At last an Indian who had been made a prisoner and had had a chance to observe their madness over gold went out and brought in a few nuggets, at which the Captain went wild.

This was what they were looking for — something to make him fight for his life and not die too easy or too soon; so they took him out to where the gold lay everywhere, led him back and bound him fast. They were having a big council to devise new means of torture when, that very same night, he dug the earth away from a sharp stone, sawed his rawhide thongs against its point and made his escape — taking the gold.

But when the great chief Cochise heard about it he sent back word that the White Eye would be back.

THE LOST DUTCHMAN MINE

All they had to do was wait and he would return to where he had seen the gold. So they kept watch on Picket Post until the Captain rode out, and this time they put him to death. But in his desk at the Post, other soldiers found a map, with a sketch showing the peak now called Weaver's Needle, almost on a line with the Four Peaks — and the gold. One after the other they disappeared into the wilderness until, as none came back, they went forth in force and drove all the Indians out of the country. But they never found the gold.

Even today the more enlightened of the gold-seekers still look for the mine south of Salt River, on a line between the Needle and the Peaks. It lies just behind the Superstition Mountains, and oldtimers, seeing its blue against the sky, still think of the brave Captain who had used it as a landmark to guide him back to the gold. From the canyon where the Apaches had kept him he had seen that sharp peak through a gap and sketched it out when he got home. But now no one knows about Weaver and his Needle, and perhaps it is just as well.

Chapter 9

STOMPEDES

WHEN JUANITO was not kidding prospectors or carrying on cowboy repartee he would tell about countless "stompedes," where he had either knocked the corner off a mountain getting away or dashed in and turned them back. His father, Dr. Jones, had been a famous storyteller and Johnny could remember, when he was a little boy, holding on to his father's long coat-tails and following him from saloon to saloon.

He had picked up a breezy style of narrative by listening to those old-timers talk, and once I got him off by himself and wrote down some of his best — after he had gone away, of course, but with the verbiage fresh in mind. It was a fine, hot day in Tempe when I saw him drop off the top of a cattle-train and head for Tom Ping's restaurant.

"Hello, Tom," he greeted, casting one leg over a stool, "gimme two orders of ham-and-eggs and a beefsteak. Get a move on, now, I'm hongry."

He made a hurried sandwich out of two slices of bread and a dill pickle and bit into it unhesitatingly.

"Hain't had nothing but bacon and flour gravy for a week," he explained. "And nothing but cigarettes since yesterday. My stomach is that shrunk up it wouldn't chamber a liver pill."

He kept on eating pickles until the ham-and-eggs arrived; after which, full at last, he sat down against the wall of the New York Store and told me all about it.

He had been out with a bunch of Mexican *vaqueros*, working for a cattle-buyer who was the champion pincher of the world. All he fed his men was bacon and flour gravy for a week. But Johnny let that go. It was for refusing to buy feed for their horses that he finally went on a strike and he collected ninety-five dollars, right there.

"I work my horse harder than I work myself," he said to the boss, "and I feed him grain and hay. If you won't pay me I'll take it out of your hide and quit with all my men, right here."

So the boss paid, but he got his money's worth, as the job was no child's play.

"I thought I'd seen wild cattle," observed Johnny, "but that bunch out in them stock-cars can git the pink ribbon anywhere. There's cows there that has never seen a man since they were branded, seven years ago. The 4L boys had to catch 'em in cattle-traps and starve 'em down before they could handle 'em at all. I wouldn't go within a mile of them longhorned Mexican critters ordinarily, but cattle are cattle, these days

123

— you have to go a hundred miles from the railroad to get anything.

"The 4L outfit had been gathering for a month, and every time they caught a new bunch they'd turn 'em into a big pasture they'd made by fencing in the canyon. They were awful proud of that pasture — it was about the size of the state of Rhode Island, I reckon — anyhow it was twelve miles square, and the brush was that high and thick you couldn't hardly see straight up. The 4L foreman told me he had eight hundred head in their by actual count, but when we rounded up the pasture we got only three hundred and forty-two.

"There's a big difference, I tell you, between a cowman and a fence-builder. The 4L boys had put all their staples on the outside of the fence, and then big steers just sifted right through and headed back for the hills. All that didn't get lost in the brush. Brush! That pasture was so brushy we couldn't ride. Had to go in there on foot and drive them out by hand, you might say. You never see such a scratched-up bunch of *vaqueros* in your life as we were when we got them rounded up. But that was only a flea-bite to what was coming to me later — I still had the seat of my pants."

Johnny has supplemented the loss of his overalls with the remnant of another pair, cut off below the knees, which he had picked up at an old camp; but his shirt was in shreds, his sombrero was battered down over his ears and only his boots were intact.

"Seems like," he complained, "I never strike it right with my shaps. When I put 'em on some outlaw bull gets after me and pretty near kills me, because I'm hobbled and can't run; and then, when I leave 'em off, I get caught in a stompede and come out stripped to the buff. The third day out we were just leaving the mouth of a canyon when there come up a tremendous big thunderstorm — one of these regular old hell-roarers. As soon as I saw it coming I threw back the leaders and we held up the herd in the open; but down the canyon the brush was so thick the birds couldn't build their nests in it.

"Well, we'd no more than got 'em stopped when the music began.

" '*Br--rump!*' she'd go, and them old cows would roll their eyes and bawl, the calves would all blat, and them old, longhorned steers would begin milling around, looking for a chance to run.

"Then she comes on to rain, and there wasn't a man in the outfit that even had a coat. Wet? I should smile — in about a minute. That rain came at us on the level, and the cattle began to drift. I heard the boys a-yelling on the other side and so I sent José Maria and the fellows I had with me to help 'em.

"About the time they got there a big, black cloud

came rolling down the canyon, shooting out thunder and lightning, and the rain turned into hailstones as big as pistol-bullets. That settled it — them cows threw up their tails and ran, with the hail bouncing off their backs two feet high.

"Well, if there was going to be a stompede I thought I might as well get in on it, but before I could catch up with the procession there came the damndest streak of lightning I ever saw in my life, right square in our faces. There was a big giant cactus up on the rim of the canyon in front of us and she busted that old *sahuaro* wide open, like a watermelon — leastwise that's what the boys told me afterwards. I wasn't interested in scenery, right then.

"I batted my eyes at the glare, and the next thing I knew old Buck had changed ends under me and was going the other way. Down the canyon to beat hell, with three hundred and forty-two wild cattle right behind us and that lovely cat-claw thicket just ahead. Maybe I didn't wish I had on my shaps — and about two more jumpers! Say, I can feel them stickers, yet!

"If there was a hole in that brush big enough to let a rabbit in I didn't see it — and I reckon Buck didn't, either. We made our plunge the first place we struck, and them cattle hit in behind like a landslide. You can't prove it by me what happened next — I went down on my horse's neck and let him do the rest. All I know is there was some fancy ducking and dodging, and I was mighty nigh dragged off twice, and then we broke into the open.

"It sounded like a million big steers was tumbling down and getting up behind; but that brush stopped 'em, all right, all right. When they came out they'd lost their steam.

"Sure! I held the whole bunch, lone-handed, and I never knowed there was anything funny about me until bimeby the boys came up. They were chasing around the other way, to head off the stompede, and when they saw me sitting there with nothing on but my boots, you might say, they pretty near died a-laughing. But you bet I made 'em pick the stickers out of me, that night!"

A triumphant smile lit up Johnny's face at the memory of this ultimate revenge and he smoked a cigarette soothingly.

"Of course we had a run every night, after that. Them cattle was so scared of lightning they'd 've stompeded if it was forty miles away, and we had to cut it out on smoking cigarettes altogether. You'd scratch a match and *sstt*, the bunch was halfway up the mountain and still a-going.

"When we got 'em down to the railroad they were that tired they couldn't hardly walk — and the conductor who run that 'commodation train told me if I didn't load them stock-cars that night he'd take 'em away and I wouldn't get no more for two weeks.

" 'I'll give you just two hours to load,' he says, 'and not a minute more.' And you bet I took him up.

"Them cars had been standing on the sidetrack for ten days while we were chasing those cows out of the pasture, and the old Con. was so hot about it I knew he'd do just what he said. There's some people think it can't be done — load three hundred and forty-two head of range cattle in two hours — but you bet I kept that engineer busy, bumping cars down to the chutes. We got most of 'em in and was working on the last car when that conductor came down the line.

" 'Time's up,' he said. 'Stop where you are!'

"But I never said nothing, just kept punching away.

" 'Hey — you,' he yells, climbing up on the fence and flashing his lantern in my eyes, 'can't you hear nothing? *Quit!*'

" 'All right,' I says. 'Be through in a minute.'

"We had 'em all loaded but one bad steer. He weighed about eleven hundred pounds, and he just naturally wouldn't go in. We put two ropes behind him and dragged him up to the door — but there he stopped. Then the Con. began to cuss.

" '*Leave* the so-and-so,' he says, swinging his lantern to start; but we kept right on working. I dropped down behind that old steer to boost and the son-of-a-gun

128

kicked me over twice. Then, by grab, I went hog-wild. I went up over his back roughshod, jumped down in front of him and slapped him in the face with my hat.

" 'Come on, you old bastard,' I hollers, and he lets out one blat and starts after me. You bet I beat the world's record, getting into that car. He was right behind me, breathing fire on them fancy overalls I'd picked up, but I ducked under the bellies of them cows and, before ary one could kick me in the face, I popped up like a weasel at the back end of the car.

" 'All right, Conductor,' I says. 'Let 'er roll!'

" 'But don't you worry about that Conductor,' — we was rolling already."

Juanito showed his teeth in a radiant grin and, reaching for his knife, began to dig the mesquite thorns out of his hands.

"Something doing every minute, that trip," he observed, shifting his seat uneasily. "I haven't had time to pick the mesquite thorns out of me yet, and the stompede was a week ago. But I tell you, man, if you want to get good and full of stickers, you do a little night-riding. Maybe I didn't get filled up good and plenty when we had a run at Monroy's corrals one night!

"I was just a kid then and if there was a stompede, or any rough riding like that, I had to be right up in front. There's been times since when I lay back and let the other fellow get the wind knocked out of him — but not then.

"We'd been gathering cattle for two or three weeks up in the Sierra Anchas, and finally got 'em down to Salt River, at old man Monroy's place. He'd built a new corral out of cottonwood logs — it was nigh on to ten feet high — and nothing would do but we had to turn them in for the night. He was proud of it and wanted it used. Of course we were glad to get them off our hands so we could make up a little sleep, but some of the boys were afraid they might bust the corral down.

" 'No can do,' says the old man in English; and, being a kid that way, I took him at his word. I had a pair of boots that fit me a little too quick anyway, so I took them off first — and that felt so good I took off my jumpers and my overalls. We wore two pair, on account of the cactus — and a pair of shaps, of course — and stretched out to be comfortable, for a change. That was a fine sleep while it lasted, but along in the night the old man's dogs heard a coyote or something and out they went — *bwooo-wooo-wooo* — right down past the corral.

"The next thing we knowed them wild, outlaw cattle had knocked one side clean out of that corral and was rolling out across the mesa — stompeded!

130

STOMPEDES

"They were in such a hurry to get away they punched the bottom out of that corral and carried the top logs on their backs, clean to the top of the hog-back. From there they run up the river a ways, and then took up Bulldog Canyon.

"Well, sir, when I heard that corral go down I took about three jumps, landed on my horse, and went biling out across the mesa to head 'em off. Some people might have stopped to put on a few clothes, but not me — I hit the wind in my undershirt and in three minutes I had more stickers in my legs than there is on a giant cactus. My horse was in on the play by that time. He knew if we didn't turn them cows back to the river we'd have some dirty work up the canyon later on, and the way he jumped gulches and smashed through the brush was scandalous.

"I didn't have anything on him but a picket-rope, anyway, so I turned him loose and spent my time dodging cactus. Down in the canyon I could hear the stompede, ripping and tearing up the wash, and you bet she sounded fierce. Them cattle was running in a solid body, just plowing their way through the cactus, and you could hear their feet clacking on the rocks like sharpening up a butcher-knife. But by that time me and old Buck was wild and we ran in on 'em, regardless.

"I've seen some stompedes in my day, but for a gen-uwine, ringtailed snorter that was the limit. Them cows was mostly outlaws anyway and they hadn't learned what a man on a horse meant, and when I rode in on 'em, yelling and swinging my picket-pin, they never moved. I crowded in on the side and tried to shove 'em over, but it was dark as a wolf's mouth down there, and the first thing I knowed the gulch took a turn and there I was, out in front of 'em!

"Say, maybe you think I wasn't scairt! My eyes bulged open until I could see like an owl, and the first thing I noticed was them long, shiny horns, getting nearer every jump. It was uphill and sandy going — and a cow can outrun a horse in the night, anyhow. I found that out in a minute. Buck began to blow and snort, and stumble a little; the canyon closed in so we couldn't get out, and I could just the same as feel them sharp feet chopping me up real fine to save on the funeral expenses — when I see a big rock ahead.

"Don't ask me how I did it — must've flew, I reckon — but when we went past that rock I dropped off and made a running high jump. When I finally came to I was sitting on a little island with nothing all around me but the heads and tails of cattle, going by like the clatter-wheels of hell."

Johnny heaved a big sigh and looked wild.

"That finished me for leading stompedes," he said. "If I can't turn 'em from the side now I let 'em go. My horse beat them cows out as soon as I got off of him

and broke up onto the high ground, and he was so scairt
he came back when I called him, just like a lost dog.
You can't tell a cow-pony nothing about stompedes —
he *knows* 'em. I don't know which was the worse stuck
up, him or me, but I got a pair of pliers and we took
turns at it — I'd pull 'em out of my legs and then out
of his. But it was many a long day before we got the
last of 'em out of us.

"Those cactus thorns are terrible and I called myself
all the names in the dictionary, but it wasn't a month
till I was leading another stompede — this time for old
Jim Barclay. He's one of the best cattlemen in the
Salt River Valley now, but then he was fresh from
Missouri and had a few things to learn. He'd been feeding punkins to them Texas dogies back there so long
that we couldn't tell him nothing. He was stocking that
big pasture of his with range cattle and there was a
fellow over on the Globe trail that had agreed to de-
liver seven hundred head at a certain place and time,
so Jim grabbed up the first men he could get and ten
of us started out.

"The cattle were there, all right, but the other outfit had driven 'em too hard and they were tired out;
so, after we'd received 'em, we left 'em on the *parada-*
ground for the night. Jim divided us up into guards,
and I went on from nine to twelve. It was a still, dark
night, with heat lightning flashing away out there over

the desert, and pretty soon the cattle started to lie down. But I'd had a little experience, if I was only a kid, and I rode out and made 'em get up.

"There's nothing like letting a steer go to sleep and then get woke up by lightning to start a stompede, but pretty soon Barclay come down from camp and rode out to where I was.

" 'Jones,' he says, kinder surprised and grieved like, 'what in the world are you doing?'

" 'Keeping 'em awake,' I says.

" 'W'y, back in Missouri where I come from,' he says, 'we'd *fire* a man for that. When a cow-brute is resting he's gaining weight. What do you want to do that for?'

" 'To keep 'em from stompeding,' I says. 'You don't want a run on your hands the first night, do you?'

"But he laughed at me — didn't know any better, then.

" 'Run!' he says, 'they can't hardly walk. Let 'em lay down, boy, and get rested.'

" 'Well, pardner,' I says, 'you're the boss, and what you say goes. All the same I'd like to bet you the drinks they'll stompede inside of an hour.'

" ' 'All right,' he says, 'and that reminds me, I came away without my canteen. Ride back and get it for me, will you?'

"It wasn't a quarter of a mile to camp and I was just

turning back when I heard a roar and knew the stompede was on. Something about a run in the night, like
that, that always makes me feel sick. It sounded like
hell had broke loose for a minute, then I throwed the
canteen away and went to it. I couldn't see nothing,
'cepting a cloud of dust, but I could hear the bulk of
the herd pounding away down the canyon and I rode
in on 'em, quartering like.

"No more leading stompedes for me — not after that
Bulldog canyon run—but being as the ground was open
and I had a start on 'em, I thought I'd take a little flier
anyway. So, when I got close to the leaders, I just un-
hooked everything and went clean across their front,
yelling like an Injun uprising. My horse was throwing
the dirt fifty feet high and I was making a big noise,
all right; but I had no idea of turning 'em. I was just
making a bluff at earning my forty a month.

"But boy, if you'll believe me, it wasn't three minutes till I had them leaders thrown back on their
haunches, just fanning the air to get away from me.
Don't know how it happened — I must have looked
fiercer than I felt. Anyhow, the bluff held good. They
turned back and went to milling and the first thing
I knew I was riding around five hundred head singing
Little Black Bull A-coming Down The Mountain like
the steam cally-ope in a circus parade.

"I held 'em, too. And while I was trying to be on

all sides of the herd at the same time, Jim Barclay and them other stiffs were riding up the canyon in the dark after two hundred head, knocking down more cactus and jumping more rock-piles than there is between here and the snow-line. They chased 'em three miles, and then some more up through the rocks; and the boys told me that Jim had me fired seventeen times over for not coming up to help.

"But when, along towards morning, they brought their little old bunch back and found me singing a bass solo to about five hundred head, he changed his mind.

"I was wore out on Little Black Bull by that time and, when I heard them fellows coming, I begun on something chesty, like this:

> " 'With my foot in the stirrup
> And my hand on the horn
> I'm the best dadburned cowboy
> That ever was born.'

"And when Jim saw them five hundred steers that he had figured the same as lost, he came around and shook hands.

" 'That's right, boy,' he says, 'you are!' And he sure set up the drinks for me when we got that herd to town.

STOMPEDES

"What starts these stompedes? Well, that's a big question. This one I was just telling you about was touched off by a dirty little sidewinder rattlesnake. He was hiding under a bunch of *galleta* grass, right close to my riding trail, and about the time them steers were sound asleep Jim turned out of the beaten path and trompled on him. Cattle are awful afraid of snakes, you know, and when that little devil rattled and struck at Jim's horse — and he jumped — the whole bunch just rose up and flew."

Johnny took off his battered sombrero and gazed philosophically at the holes in the crown.

"All these big stompedes," he said, "come off at night, and the worst ones happen when the cows have been asleep. I used to think them cattle had bad dreams and woke up scared. You know how kids will dream they're falling over a thousand-foot cliff and wake up yelling bloody murder? Well, what's the matter with cows doing the same thing?

"There's always a lot of outlaws along — steers that have been roped and manhandled and maybe left out a night or two, with their legs tied and the coyotes trying to chew their ear. Just think what a nightmare that would make! And then, while this outlaw is dreaming that the coyotes are eating on him, some other steer stretches a cramp out of his leg and jabs him in the back. Would he wake up running? Well, say!

137

"An old Apache medicine man told me one time that these stompedes are caused by bad spirits, and he offered for one beef-critter to drive these Injun devils away. Our cattle were running bad at the time and we pretty near took him up, but I reckon the old boy was just meat-hungry. All the same, there's something mysterious and spooky about it and I come pretty nigh knowing when it's going to happen to cows.

"When they've got these stompede devils in 'em, anybody can tell it. As soon as the sun goes down their eyes begin to burn like bull's-eye lanterns. And when you ride in among 'em you can just *feel* that crazy, locoed spirit. Then if a man's hat blows off, or a horse stumbles or some guy lights a match, the whole bunch will hit the wind — and if you happen to be in the way, God help you!

"Do people get *killed* in them stompedes? That's right, pardner, more than you'd think; but we don't talk about it. You know Jose Maria Roblero, that just come in on that train. He had all the curl took out of his hair in about a minute, and one of his best friends got killed. There were twenty-seven of 'em, all Mexicans, and they undertook to drive a herd of range steers from Tucson to Willcox. The country down there is all open — you wouldn't find a tree big enough to climb in thirty miles.

"It's bad enough to have stompedes up in these

rocky canyons; but a man has got a chance, anyhow. He can jump up on a boulder or maybe climb a palo verde if he isn't too particular about thorns; but when you roll out of your blankets and try to outrun fifteen hundred locoed steers, you feel kinder creepy. Well, that's what Joe did.

"It was right in the middle of a big plain and forty miles from nowhere. The night guards were holding the herd and all the rest were asleep when the whole bunch stompeded — straight for the wagon. Jose heard the roar and felt the ground tremble under him. Then he jumped up and run with the rest. It wasn't any use — but nothing else was, either — and them steers were whirling down on 'em like death and destruction.

"There was over twenty *vaqueros* sleeping around that wagon and they all got up and run like rabbits — all but one man. There was one old Mexican that had his nerve with him, you bet. He stood up in his blankets and, when the stompede was about fifty yards away, he scratched a match! Only chance he had, but that match did the business.

"When the leaders saw it flash they flew back and side-jumped, and then the whole herd opened out like it was split with a jackknife. Old Manuel cupped his hands and held that match steady, and before it burned down to his fingers the stompede had passed. Them steers never touched the chuck-wagon, and when they caught up with Jose Maria — which was in about forty jumps — they went by him in a solid wall. There was just one fellow killed, and that was Joe's friend. He got rattled and run sideways. But hell's bells, man, that's coming too close!"

Chapter 10

THE PLEASANT VALLEY WAR

WE WERE visited a few days later by a band of Apache women, sent ahead by their menfolks to gather some mescal hearts and put them in a pit to roast. These yucca hearts are very sweet after being baked with hot rocks for three days, and it is the custom of the men to follow along and have a big time helping to eat them. The women were headed by Old Susie, the official chaperon of the party, who had a butcher-knife in the leg of her moccasin, and as they were out of grub Johnny gave them a shoulder of beef.

They were all known to the Mexicans, who lived on the edge of the Reservation and were on friendly terms with the bucks, but at some time they had been frightened by white men, for they were as shy and wary as deer. And Susie, though she was a hard looker, was positively censorious. The prettiest girl among them was Grace Pelchu, a Carlisle graduate who spoke good English; but after coming back home there was nothing for her to do and she married a worthless buck.

After harvesting their mescal hearts and burying them in the pit to roast they returned to our camp at Cane Spring and Old Susie asked for the hide of the beef which we had killed a few days before. They wanted it to make soles for their buckskin moccasins; and Johnny, who was eating, told her where to find it. But what they were really hanging around for was to get something more to eat, and Susie did not hunt very hard; until at last, impatiently, he got up and motioned her into the brush.

"No," she said, shaking her head.

"*Ven* — come!" he coaxed; and then Susie went on the warpath.

"No!" she yelled, reaching for her butcher-knife, and Johnny strode ahead in disgust. Snatching up the wrinkled hide he heaved it towards her and went back to his interrupted meal. All the Mexicans began to laugh and make sly remarks, but Juanito was sore at having his motives misconstrued, and when Susie asked for some meat he told her to go away. To all the other women he gave a chunk of beef, but Susie had to put up quite a talk before he would give her anything.

When the women were in a more friendly mood, which was right after they had eaten their beef, I took some photographs of Grace Pelchu and her baby, which was bound up in its cradle like a Della Robbia *bambino*. It made a very pretty picture and I felt sorry for the poor girl; for, with all her education, she had gone back to the blanket and half the time had nothing to eat. When the men came trooping in it just made things worse, for all they brought was a rabbit which

Grace Pelchu, a Carlisle Graduate, with her Baby.

Sheep!

one had shot with his .22 rifle. They were big, rugged fellows, weighing around two hundred pounds, and as they would not work by the day they were idle most of the time. But give them a contract and they would clear more land for a dollar than a white man would for ten.

Indian-like they rode by without a word, but when one of them came back to bum some tobacco he set the whole camp in a furore.

"*Muchos borregos* — many sheep," he observed, waving his hand back towards Cottonwood Wash; and after Johnny had got through questioning him he went off down the trail at a gallop. The sheep had moved in on the lower range and were feeding off the country for miles. The question was, where was El Yeem, the Ranger, who had promised to keep them off?

When I rode down the next day I found Johnny at the top of a telephone pole, hollering through a field receiver to the Forest Office at Roosevelt. But Jim was not there, nobody knew anything about him and there was no ranger to send in his place; and Johnny's last words to the Supervisor were calculated to burn him up.

So far as I know Jim never did return to take up his neglected duties, and over a hundred thousand sheep went across the range, feeding the grass down before them. The sheepmen were out in force, determined to

143

fight their way through but taking their time about that. They were frank to state that a Sheep Trail two miles wide wouldn't hold the half of their sheep; and the Government, by restricting them to such a narrow passageway, had done them a rank injustice. It could sue them if it wanted to and put them off the range; but this time they were going *through*, and no bunch of cowmen could stop them.

They went through, all right, and on up the Tonto; but when they came back there was another Ranger on the job, and he kept them to the Trail. He was a "fountain-pen boy" from the East, but a fine-looking, upstanding kid who was having the time of his life. Everybody liked him, and Don Pancho said the Reenger was going to stay there always. He was in love with Arizona and a girl up on the Verde, and he was going to protect them from the sheep.

This was good news for the cowmen, who were paying thirty-five cents a head grazing fee and beginning to wonder what it brought them. The sheep were paying only six cents and, coming through twice a year, they had left the Trail as slick as your hand. Also a wide strip on both sides, for the Mexican sheepherders all had the same orders: Feed my sheep!

Regardless of signs they would turn off the Trail anywhere; and by the time the Ranger had got one herd back the others would be over the line. It was asking a great deal of one man to expect him to patrol the whole Trail, but the fountain-pen boy had done his best and in the spring the grass was fine. They had had lots of rain and, while the range still looked bare, it was hoped that a few years more would bring it back into shape.

But the ridges were still sticking out like the ribs on a starved-down horse, and every time it rained the trenches grew deeper where the sheep had left their trails. A million dollars wouldn't block all those gulches and restore the furrowed flats, and if the range was not protected the whole watershed would be washed away. Already the great lake behind the Roosevelt Dam was filling up like a beaver-meadow, restricting by so much the amount of water it would impound to provide against the next big drouth. It was a serious matter for the farmers of the Salt River Valley and, as their diversion dams were being silted up, they could be depended upon to protest.

Or that's what the Four Peaks cattlemen thought when they rode in for the spring round-up — but the new Ranger was not there. Competition was fierce on the Verde, and he had moved his headquarters up the river in order to be nearer the girl. The boys were all laughing, but of one thing they felt certain — when the sheep came through he would be there with bells, and make them keep to the Trail. He had done it when they came down and he would do it coming back, and that was all they asked for — protection.

John Gilliland had had to catch a mountain lion with his rope on account of being without a gun, and he had gone back to packing his six-shooter. He had been wearing one so long his clothes didn't fit, anyway; but he had nearly lost twenty dollars. That was the bounty on lions. His dogs had jumped one on the upper range and, when it crawled along the face of a cliff, he had gone up after it with rocks. When the shelf came to an end and the lion turned back John had had to creep into a narrow pocket to let the critter get by.

But twenty dollars was too much to lose and, when his dogs chased it into a cave, Gilliland followed and smoked it out. It was just his luck to be caught out on a ledge again, and when the lion charged towards him he jumped up and caught hold of a root, hanging on until it went by. The dogs took after it and ran it into another cave; and this time, when he smoked it out, John was waiting up above with the rope. He lassed it around the neck, jerked it over the edge of the cliff and held on to it until he choked it to death. But that was working too hard and now he was carrying a gun.

He was feeling very jolly on account of having snared a wild horse the day before and, one story lead-

146

ing to another, he got around to the Pleasant Valley War. That is a subject you can't bring up yourself, but if one of the survivors wants to talk about it, it is all right to listen. Nobody else was around and, in his corrugated-iron cabin, John stretched himself on the bunk and gave me the low-down on the feud.

It all started when a lawyer named Stimson made a trade for some Mormon cattle and put them in Tonto Basin, at that time practically uninhabited. Pleasant Valley lies under the rim of the Mogollon Plateau, which breaks off suddenly to the south, leaving a very beautiful country, then only accessible by trails. There were 1500 head, the brand was a plain T on the ribs and hip; and it was not long, with an iron like that, before rustlers began to burn it over.

Prominent among these were the Tewksbury and Graham families — the Tewksburys half-breed Indians from Northern California, the Grahams coming from Texas. They were working together, stealing cattle from Stimson, but the Tewksburys had brought some fine horses with them and were raising more on the side. The Grahams were big, handsome men, but, being Texans, they had a color prejudice against the Tewksburys, some of whom were very dark. But they were all dead shots and when the two families tangled and fought it out, the last of the Tewksbury's killed the last of the Grahams. Then he got on his best horse

147

and, riding by relays, went from Tempe to Young P. O. in Pleasant Valley, in time to establish an alibi.

It was the biggest feud in the history of Arizona if not in all the West, and the people in Pleasant Valley were still carrying guns and walking softly when I visited there in 1916. The only man that would talk was the sole survivor of another fighting family which had been wiped out during the war, and he didn't care much what happened. He just wanted to tell the world that he had been railroaded to prison for something he had never done; and, from the way he talked, I believe it.

The Tewksburys and Grahams were doing fine until they fell out among themselves. After that it was law-courts, shootings and ambushes until towards the end, Gila County and Yavapai County both went broke and left them to fight it out. There were deeds of heroism and noble devotion, by the women as well as the men, and every boy big enough to carry a gun hung on his six-shooter and went to it.

When Gilliland begins his story the Tewksburys and Grahams were still friends and he was working for Stimson who, being a lawyer, had the idea that the law would protect his cows.

"One morning," John said, "I was out with an old Mexican when we came across a yearling that had just been killed and only the tenderloin cut out. We

148

followed the horse-tracks to down near a house where I knew Ed Tewksbury was staying, but I lost the trail in a thicket and went back to look for the ears. I found one, with the Stimson earmark, cut off and thrown in the grass; so the next morning I went back to the house to tell Ed I knew what was up. I wasn't looking for any trouble and let a sixteen-year-old cousin ride along. But when we got within two hundred yards of the house I saw three men out in front, watching us — Ed Tewksbury and two of the Graham boys.

"As soon as they saw me they began to talk and whisper together, and I could see they were getting excited. Then, when I was about thirty feet away, the two Grahams jumped behind an old forge and pulled their six-shooters. At the same time Ed, who was standing in the open, drew his pistol and fired. I pulled mine, but at the first shot my horse, that was young and half-broken, began to buck and whirl around. They were all three shooting at me, but they only hit me once.

"I was leaning over when a bullet went into my back and lodged in my shoulder, but I never knew I was hit. Thought I'd bumped my crazy-bone against the horn while my horse was pitching around. I only shot twice, but if I'd had a good horse under me I would have got Tewksbury. At the first shot I told my cousin to run, but he had no more than started when a bullet hit him in the back. It came out in front, high up.

" 'I'm killed!' he hollered and fell on his face. When I rode away I looked down at him and he seemed dead; but after the fight the Tewksburys took him nine miles to their home ranch and got a doctor, who cured him.

"When all their six-shooters were empty, and me still fighting my horse, one of the Grahams hollered out:

. . " 'I'll go to the house and get my Winchester — I'll bet I can git you with that!'

"But by the time he got his rifle I was too far away. I rode thirty miles to Tonto, where a friend cut the bullet out of my back with a dull razor and I went on down to Phoenix. I told Stimson he was being robbed but before he could do anything about it the Tewksburys and Grahams went to Prescott and swore out a warrant against me for attempted murder. There were nine of them. Stimson telegraphed up and had them all arrested, and at the trial they all swore they were present when I made my unprovoked assault. But it came out they were perjuring themselves, and the judge turned me loose.

Then the Tewksburys and Grahams, that had been in the cattle-stealing business together, fell out over one of the Grahams making love to the wife of one of the Tewksburys; and at the trial that followed they went together all the time, although Graham's wife was right there. That gave Stimson his chance and he offered the Grahams a hundred head of cattle to swear the Tewksburys into prison. But they overdid it again, told too much and nearly swore themselves in.

"The evidence failed to convict and the Tewksburys had the *Grahams* tried for perjury. This failed too and the judge practically told them to go home and fight it out. The county warrants were no good, it was two hundred miles back and forth every time a deputy went out, and either side would swear to a lie. So the Grahams took to the high mountains, and both sides lay in wait on the hills above the other ones' houses to shoot any man that came out.

"The first killing was made by the Grahams. They got together all their friends and watched the Tewksbury house; and when, early in the morning, two of them went out for their horses they shot them down from the hills. The rest of the men ran out the back way and got into the rocks but the women went out to bring in the bodies, before the wild hogs got to them. The hogs didn't eat them, as most people believe, but it is a fact that the Grahams turned the women back by shooting all around them.

"After that the Tewksburys ambushed the Grahams when they came in to the store for their mail, and the hills were full of men watching the trails. Many strangers passing through the country were shot on general principles or to keep them from joining the other side, and a bunch of Hash Knife gunmen came down and tried to clean up on the Tewksburys. But it worked the other way. A boy of eighteen jumped out among them with a carbine and, while their horses were bucking, he shot two men out of the saddle, wounded three or four more and never got a scratch. He was just Indian enough to figure it out.

"I stayed out of it for a while and then went in with a Dutchman who had been driven away from his mine. He gave me and another fellow equal shares to protect him, but we didn't have to do any fighting. We saw one old, simple-minded man shot at from the buttes. The bullets struck all around him and he skipped the country. We saw another armed man chasing some cattle up a gulch and held him up when he came over the rim, but he swore he didn't know anybody or anything, so we finally turned him loose.

"After the war was over I gathered Stimson's cattle for him — what were left; but most of them had been stolen by the Tewksburys and Grahams. Of the nine men who swore against me at Prescott eight were killed in the fighting and the other one died later. When I see these sheepherders with their little old guns ——"

Chapter 11

"FEED MY SHEEP!"

JOHN didn't say what he would do but, in the Pleasant Valley War, Black Hat, the fighting sheepman, had lost ten thousand head and two herders, and the Mexicans never forgot it. The old Dead Line was just west of Jack Steward's cabin where Gilliland made his headquarters and, while the sheepherders crossed the Line everywhere else, they never crossed it there. All the orders they had were: "Feed my sheep!" So they used a little discretion.

That showed they were not so ignorant as they seemed. They were constitutionally unable to keep in that Sheep Trail, but they always kept clear of John. He knew a quick way of making them walk a chalk-line, but his boss was a man of peace and he never gave the word. It was a National Forest now and they were paying a big grazing fee to be protected in their rights, so why not let the Government do it?

Our Ranger was absent when we started for Cane Spring, but he had turned the sheep once and he could do it again. It was only that the competition up on the Verde was fierce and he had to ride herd on the girl. So, while the river was high and the sheep couldn't cross anyway, it was decided to begin the round-up on the upper range and, accidentally on purpose, be down near the Dead Line when the sheep men began moving north.

Now that the flood-gates were in — holding back the rush of water from the winter rains and letting it out in the spring — it made Salt River a veritable barrier against the sheep. Always before, taking advantage of some dry spell or cold weather in the mountains, a few herders would push their flocks across, losing some of the weak ones in the swift water but getting the first chance at the feed. Now they had to wait until the farmers down below ceased to use so much water for their fields.

Everybody was satisfied that the Ranger would be there when they crossed, and the rodeo was in full swing when I left Cane Spring and started for town.

The grass was fine when I got down on the Cotton-wood, but when I approached the old Jones place I smelled sheep a mile away. They were coming up the wash in a solid phalanx, heading into the upper range, and our fountain-pen Ranger was not there. Even the herders disappeared when they saw me coming. But the sheep! They kept right on.

At the mouth of Cottonwood Canyon the ground was fed off bare; and Johnny Jones' pasture, which he was keeping for his horses, was swept clean and trampled flat. In the round corral, where the branding was always done, a gang of Mexican herders were holding their sheep while they counted them through the gate. No body could understand a word of English, but when the cowboys came down and had to inhale that sheep-manure very likely they would be on the prod.

This was none of my business, of course. I was heading for San Carlos, where the Texas cowboys held forth, and did not intend to come back. But, hoping to get a picture or two, I headed up the river to where the crossing was going on. The river was high — I doubted if I could cross it — but some enterprising sheepman had figured out a way of beating the flood.

Against the wall of Bulldog Cliff, where the river rushes out of the Box Canyon, a herd of sheep was being held while, a cut at a time, the leaders were put across. Long strips of tarpaulin were stretched behind a bunch of them, and they were dragged down a slippery place to a jump-off on the edge of the water. There, with a final heave, they were flung into the river, where they could either swim or drown.

But sheep are a poor, timid lot, perfectly capable of floating down the stream until they sink or die, and the herders had borrowed Pancho Monroy's goats to lead them across. They struck out bravely for the opposite side, and half the sheep fell in behind. The rest turned back, intending to land in the brush below, but a line of naked Mexicans rushed out and, yelling and throwing clubs, forced them to swim across.

Some sank and never came up but the sheep-owner drove his men on, riding in on his mule to help the herd across, stripping down and working with the rest. He was a heroic figure, like a bearded water-god, and when he met one of the Mexicans who was feeling playful he would seize him by the hair and shove his head under water. Then they would all laugh, like the barbarians they were, and turn back to get more sheep. The lambs they took away from their bawling mothers and, placing them twenty at a time in a huge sheet of canvas, floated them to the other side. Then they heaved in the ewes while they were still calling after them and, naturally, they kept on across.

It was a magnificent picture of man in his conflict with the forces of nature, but I decided not to take my photographs. My big, bearded Triton had sighted me on the bluff and was shouting across the river and pointing; and, even if I had been a Ranger, I should have hesitated to oppose his will.

He was going across, I could see that; and, though the shallows down the river were spotted with dead sheep, nothing would turn him back. The rest of the herd would reach land, thanks to Don Pancho's goats, and have the first chance at the grass which was growing along the Trail. But they would not follow the

"Feed My Sheep!"

Trail. Band after band was heading for the upper range; and I could imagine Johnny Jones, a couple of days later, shouting imprecations over the field telephone that would make the stenographers blush.

A chain is as strong as its weakest link, and our fountain-pen Ranger had failed us. But the next day, as I took the stage to Roosevelt, I wondered what had kept him away. Had he had his paws greased and conveniently absented himself, or had he been bluffed out? It would take quite a man to stand up to all those sheepmen and tell them what to do and not to do. Yet, after all that the cowboys had said, I hesitated to believe he was a weakling. He might have gone up the Verde to see his girl but — well, I decided to stop over at Roosevelt and talk with the Forest Supervisor.

There is nothing like going to headquarters when you want some real information and this Supervisor had lots of it — all carefully arranged in files, which he consulted on every occasion. When I told him I had just come up from Salt River and wondered why the sheep were off their Trail, I got everything but what I asked for. I was given all the figures on the use of Verde salt and other technical subjects; but as to why the Ranger, as the particular time he was most needed, had suddenly dropped out of sight, I got everything but an answer.

It finally became apparent that I wasn't going to get

157

an answer — not unless I hollered for it. At that he lost his patience and informed me that the Ranger had been recalled to headquarters to attend to some very important business on the eastern side of the Reservation. He was engaged in the performance of his duty and, on his return, would be sent back to the Verde. Meanwhile I should remember that, while the Four Peaks cattlemen were entitled to every consideration, they were not the only people on the Forest. There were other stockmen who were equally entitled to their rights.

That was the answer, but I did not pass it on to Johnny. Sooner or later he would find out that, like most Arizona cowboys, he was destined to spend the rest of his life fighting sheep.

Now a more just-minded Forest Service has found a way of keeping the sheep on the Trail, but Juanito is not here to see it. He died of the flu a few years later, shortly after his marriage when he had everything to live for, and his old range is divided into Forest allotments and mostly under wire.

The fighting sheepmen who used to move in on him have been tamed by having their permits revoked, and sheep-and-cattle wars are unknown. Not until they get down on the desert, off the Forest, are they free to roam the public domain, and for forty miles there is not a blade of grass left to remind them of the good old days.

"Feed My Sheep!"

The brave old days, when a cowboy could throw his hat into the air and follow whichever way it sailed, sure of getting a job! They are still just as good men and just as good riders, but the prolonged drouths have destroyed the open range, and the methods of working cattle have changed. Now a couple of cowboys will put their horses in a trailer, hook it onto a truck and drive forty miles along the fence. Then they will round up some pasture, brand the calves, and get back to the ranch before dark.

I can remember one morning, not so very long ago, when as the Cherrycow boys rode out on the circle we cut the track of an automobile and the wagon-boss said:

"William Riggs has been by here."

"How do you know it was Riggs?" I asked.

"Because," he answered, "he owns the only Ford car in the Sulphur Springs Valley."

It was only twenty-six years ago and yet, where there were then 25,000 head of cattle on the range, there are less than 3,000 now, and lots of Fords. They haul their feeders to the railroad in trucks and, when the guests from the dude ranches want to see a herd of cattle, they have to drive to the Mexican Line — when they cross. The cattlemen have figured it out that it takes too much flesh off their animals to drive them to market over the trails.

159

Everything is mechanized, like modern business, but the boys say their cow-ponies like it. As they glide grandly along the highway they look up at the high peaks, over which they have been chasing cows, and seem to say:

"This is the life! They give us a ride home now, after our hard work is done. It was different in the old days."

THE END